Conversations About Being a Teacher

**CORWIN
PRESS**

The Corwin Press logo—a raven striding across an open book—represents the union of courage and learning. Corwin Press is committed to improving education for all learners by publishing books and other professional development resources for those serving the field of K–12 education. By providing practical, hands-on materials, Corwin Press continues to carry out the promise of its motto: **"Helping Educators Do Their Work Better."**

Foreword by Thomas R. Giblin

Conversations About Being a Teacher

J. Victor McGuire
with Carolyn S. Duff

CORWIN PRESS
A Sage Publications Company
Thousand Oaks, California

Portions of the text were written in collaboration with Carolyn S. Duff of Ft. Collins, CO, and are used here with her permission.

The Teacher Effective Awareness Stretch illustration is based on a model created by Dr. Chuck Luna, Rocky Mountain Intercultural Institute, of Lafayette, CO, and is adapted here with his permission.

For information:

Corwin Press
A Sage Publications Company
2455 Teller Road
Thousand Oaks, California 91320
www.corwinpress.com

Sage Publications Ltd.
1 Oliver's Yard
55 City Road
London EC1Y 1SP
United Kingdom

Sage Publications India Pvt. Ltd.
B-42, Panchsheel Enclave
Post Box 4109
New Delhi 110 017 India

Printed in the United States of America

Library of Congress Cataloging-in-Publication Data

McGuire, J. Victor.
Conversations about being a teacher / J. Victor McGuire with Carolyn S. Duff; foreword by Thomas R. Giblin.
    p. cm.
Includes bibliographical references and index.
ISBN 1-4129-0598-2 (cloth) — ISBN 1-4129-0599-0 (pbk.)
    1. Teachers—Training of—United States—Case studies.
2. Teacher effectiveness—United States—Case studies. 3. Mentoring in education—United States—Case studies. I. Duff, Carolyn S., 1941- II. Title.
LB1715.M22 2005
371.1—dc22
                                            2004004600

04   05   06   07   10   9   8   7   6   5   4   3   2   1

Acquisitions Editor:	Faye Zucker
Editorial Assistant:	Stacy Wagner
Production Editor:	Melanie Birdsall
Copy Editor:	Elizabeth Budd
Typesetter:	C&M Digitals (P) Ltd.
Proofreader:	Kristin Bergstad
Indexer:	Michael Ferreira
Cover Designer:	Tracy E. Miller
Graphic Designer:	Lisa Miller

Contents

Foreword

It's always a treat when I pick up an educational textbook, and because I can't put it down, I end up reading it from cover to cover in one sitting. That's what happened when I first read the manuscript for *Conversations About Being a Teacher*; I was totally captivated by the engaging story of a young teacher and an aging professor.

Dr. McGuire has blended the ingredients of a traditional textbook with the elements of a contemporary novel, creating a "nextbook" that will leave you wondering why more textbooks don't adopt this novel (in both senses of the word!) format. Before you think that the book has been written to appeal only to the MTV generation, I should offer that, having shared and talked about it with a wide range of young and experienced teachers, everyone has been enthusiastic about both the content and the delivery.

Each chapter of the book you are about to read consists of a charming conversation between the eager but inexperienced Tonya, and her chosen mentor, the irascible education professor Dr. Michaels. The conversations are animated, insightful, smile-producing journeys into what it takes to be a teacher. Note taking is optional, but you may find yourself underlining a statement or two or putting a paper clip on a page for future reference. The dialogue contains powerful strategies for understanding and tackling the complexities of teaching.

While Tonya and Dr. Michaels are only two members among a cast of thousands that we could call upon to converse about teaching, their story showcases the critical factor associated with teacher effectiveness: *building relationships.* At every level and within every dimension of education, from kindergarten classrooms to school board meetings, from preservice classrooms to professional development seminars, we know the importance of effective relationships. Granted, relationships are always a work in progress, as Tonya and Dr. Michaels' story illustrates, but, as their story also shows, once a relationship is established, teaching and learning blossom.

The book speaks clearly to today's prospective teachers as well as to reflective and introspective veterans who seek further development within their chosen field. For those working toward teacher certification and for the newest members of the profession, the conversations provide a refreshing introduction to many critical elements of teaching. Teacher educators, principals, supervisors, and other leaders in education know that caring, respect, and commitment are critical, but they are removed from the situations in which Tonya must apply them as a beginning teacher. For more experienced teachers, the conversations will be a walk down memory lane and a reminder of why they decided to become teachers in the first place. Those memories will reinforce what they have grown to believe is important and rejuvenate them as classroom teachers.

Does this "nextbook" really work as a textbook or is it more faithfully a novel about education? Well, it is both. Either way you slice it, the result is good: Dr. McGuire's book will promote much needed reflective conversations about teaching. Those in the textbook camp can use the topics to discuss the essential elements of effective teaching, brainstorm other factors that improve teaching, talk about which aspects make sense to them and which are questionable, and write down their beliefs about teaching. Those in the novel camp can reflect on the story, discuss the strengths and weaknesses of the characters, project what kind of teacher Tonya will be, and even begin their own sequel to the story, perhaps imagining Tonya as an aging professor meeting a young teacher for the first time—thirty-five years from now!

With *Conversations About Being a Teacher,* Dr. McGuire has taken a bold stand in defining what he believes to be important. He has started the conversation; now it is up to us to continue it!

—Thomas R. Giblin, PhD

Chair and Professor
Department of Education and
Human Development
SUNY College at Brockport

Acknowledgments

I have had many teachers over the last 40-plus years who have played a key and important part in my personal and professional development. I would like to acknowledge those individuals.

My mother and father Louis and Bernice McGuire, my first teachers, who gave me lessons before I knew what a lesson was!

Cheryl Butler McGuire and Casandra Butler, my wife and daughter, who give me unconditional love and support and the freedom to do what I love to do—teach.

Carolyn Duff, one of my biggest supporters, thank you for all of your insight, wisdom, and direction. You should be proud of what we did I am!

Mr. Jeff Williams, my big brother, who kept me out of trouble.

Mr. and Mrs. Bill Grunewald and Sandy, thank you for showing me what family was all about.

Mr. Robert Hyde, my fourth- and fifth-grade teacher who taught me to "think before you act."

Ruth E. Harvey, my cottage parent at Allendale School for Boys, who introduced me to discipline, consistency, and caring.

Mr. Eustice, who taught me the etiquette and skill of archery, my first sport.

Mr. Bob Grennert, who taught me my basketball jump shot when I was age 12.

Mr. Paul Noe, who taught me peaceful patience.

Mrs. Chloe Hendrickson, who gave me a place to be, and also a place to grow.

Mr. and Mrs. Wapon, my first high school teachers, a summer of transition.

Mrs. Bea Ano, who gave me a sense of direction when I was headed down the wrong path.

Mrs. Lipski, my first real English teacher.

Mr. Sandburg, high school track coach, who showed me what being part of a team is all about. A great motivator and great coach.

Mr. Wayne Parthun, who has been one of my best supporters for more than 30 years. Without his direction, college would have not been possible.

Dr. Dudley and Lowell Dodd of Doane College, my first teachers of education, whose dedication, direction, and purpose was and will continue to play an important role in my development as a teacher.

Dr. Charles Railsback, my first and only teacher of theatre, who set the stage for my professional direction.

Mr. Fred Beilie, not just my college track coach, who also set the example of dedication and leadership.

Father Ivan Vap, who gave me my first job out of college; thank you for giving this beginning teacher an opportunity to teach.

Dr. Rich Feller, a college professor who has taught me what true friendship is about.

Dr. Timothy Houlton, who taught me what giving of oneself is all about.

Corwin Press extends its thanks to the following reviewers for their contributions to this book:

Michelle Barnea, Educational Consultant, Millburn, NJ

Sue Braun, Rousseau Elementary School, Lincoln, NE

Marta Cruz-Janzen, Florida Atlantic University, Boca Raton, FL

Thomas R. Giblin, SUNY College at Brockport, NY

Shirley Miles, Academy School District 20, Colorado Springs, CO

Karyn Wright, Clark County School District, Las Vegas, NV

About the Author

J. Victor McGuire, PhD, is a 25-year veteran of the education field. As an alumnus of the international Fulbright–Hayes Scholarship organization, Dr. McGuire uses his global educational experience to inspire and motivate the next generation of teachers. Recently, he founded the National Association for Beginning Teachers (beginning teachers.org), which offers service and support to preservice and beginning teachers. He has authored and published a variety of practitioner-based educational books and is the editor of *Inspire,* a magazine for beginning teachers. Currently, Dr. McGuire is on the faculty in the College of Education at the University of Nevada, Las Vegas.

If you are interested in having a conversation about teaching with Dr. McGuire, please visit www.teachingconversations.com.

CONVERSATION ONE

Mission and Vision

Make your life a mission—not an intermission.

—Arnold Glasgow

T onya hit the door to the stairwell with her right shoulder and began taking the stairs two or three at a time. She was late for her appointment with Dr. Michaels, full professor in the education department. She had never been in one of his classes, although many preservice students who had couldn't stop talking about his ideas, his stories, and his broad-based knowledge. This man had been making an impact on new teachers for years, probably decades, and she didn't intend to miss the opportunity to learn from him. As she crashed, again shoulder first, through the stairwell door to the third floor, she caught up to herself in a moment of hesitation. Her friend who had known him as his high school civics teacher extolled his involvement and caring and his enthusiasm for his subject matter. Some of his recent students, however, complained that he seemed distant. A guy named Steve in his current class described him as brutally direct and irritable.

The professor's door was open a few inches, but she knocked anyway, reluctant yet determined. "I'm sorry I'm late. I'm Tonya Simmons, and I have an appointment with you—with Dr. Michaels."

"I've been waiting for twenty minutes, Ms. Simmons." Dr. Michaels paused and looked straight at her, then turned and sat in the chair behind his desk. He gestured for her to take a chair across from him. Over a spread of manila files, sets of papers, and assorted books feathered with slips of paper, he concentrated his gaze. "Do you keep your students waiting," he asked, "or do you get to class on time?"

"I apologize, Dr. Michaels." Tonya acted appropriately contrite but didn't budge from her purpose. "I'm student teaching at Peterson, and my master teacher wanted to talk to me about our next unit before we introduce it on Monday. I got here as soon as I could."

The professor kept her standing and let her stew. "Consider all the possibilities before you make commitments, Ms. Simmons. I might think you don't respect my time."

"Originally we had planned to meet at lunch," she went on, resolutely defending herself, although she wished she had gotten off to a better start. "I waited in the teacher's lounge until almost the end of the period. Just as I was about to leave for class, she called from the administrative building and asked if we could get together right when school ended. I never got lunch!"

"You have missed lunch before and you will miss lunch again," he commented without sympathy. "So, now that you're here, why don't you tell me why you are here?"

Very little intimidated Tonya Simmons. All through her school career, she had been considered bright, assertive, and up to a challenge. She was tight with details of her personal life, but friendly and a good listener. In high school, she had been one of three African American girls on the school's winning basketball team, and she valued winning. Her parents were divorced; during high school she lived with her mother, a surgical nurse, and her younger brother. Her father, an engineer with an international rubber company, lived in the same city with his new wife and their three children. Tonya had managed college mostly on her own with scholarships, grants, loans, and various on-campus jobs. After graduating, she taught English in Japan for a year before returning to school for her teaching degree. Each new experience added to her confidence, although she was never as sure of herself as others took her to be. Approaching Dr. Michaels for input on being a teacher had taken both nerve and humility, but once Tonya made a decision, she stuck with it. So here she was—and she was going to make the best of it, regardless of the unfortunate start.

"I finish my student teaching in June," Tonya responded to the professor, "and I am fortunate to have a job at Sequoia High School next fall." Tonya scanned the office for a chair but remained standing. "I will be certified, but I don't really feel as ready as I would like to be. I've never been able to take one of your classes, and everyone says what a wonderful professor you were and how well you helped them prepare to teach." Tonya looked up at Dr. Michaels and stated simply and directly, "I want to be an excellent teacher, and I hope you can help me."

"They remember the teacher I was," Dr. Michaels responded with a determined smile, forming a steeple with his index fingers. "An interesting way you put things, Ms. Simmons. Curious that you would seek out an old 'has-been' as your teaching guide."

His goad annoyed Tonya, but she had been prepared for Michaels' irascibility. She began to protest that she hadn't meant anything negative, but the professor interrupted before she could explain herself. "Whether you meant it or not," he continued in a comfortable baritone, "there may be some truth to it. I've been in this game for a long time. Teaching is what I do. 'Has-been' or not, I still have responsibilities here. I can't be giving one-on-one seminars for everyone who comes through the door."

"Oh, I understand." In a softer and less defensive tone, Tonya restated her petition. "I thought maybe you could just give me some suggestions from your experience, maybe some books or articles to read, some teachers to observe."

"Think of it this way, Ms. Simmons. Here you are, in my office at—let me see; now it's 4:15 on a Friday afternoon. You want something from me?" Dr. Michaels leaned back in his chair and pulled open a file drawer. He took out a box of bread sticks, shook a few forward, and offered them to Tonya. She watched, but remained motionless and quiet.

"You told me you missed lunch. You must be hungry. Take one, Ms. Simmons. Or take two or three. I'm offering them because they are what I have to give. They will stave off your hunger for a while. What do you think? Will the bread sticks do the trick?"

Tonya wasn't sure if Michaels was being sarcastic or if this were some sort of a test. She decided to go along with the game. "They would help me stop being hungry," she responded, "but I don't get what you're after."

"Well, think of it this way." The professor knew he had hooked her attention and leaned back in his chair, tapping the wooden arm with his index finger. "If every time you come to my office and sit down at my table, I offer you bread sticks, would you be satisfied?" He waited for her to take up the challenge.

"I guess I would get pretty sick of them. I'd want something more," she paused, as if grappling with her options. "Maybe I'd want water or fruit or cheese or something."

"Absolutely." Dr. Michaels sat up straight then leaned forward on his elbows, looking right at Tonya. "Then it becomes your responsibility to bring something to the table also." He seemed pleased with himself and went on. "The more we bring to the table, the better the meal we will have. Think of that with your students, too. You, the teacher, will begin with the bread sticks—basic but incomplete without other contributions. Your students will be required to bring stuff as well. You provide the syllabus, the textbook; they come in with enthusiasm, with questions, with new ideas. You add to the banquet with your caring about them, your experiences, and your sense of humor. Everyone ends up with a full plate!"

"So you are saying that if I want to learn something from you, to get a full plate, I have to contribute something too, right?" Tonya had caught the metaphor and was interested to see where the professor was going.

"Right," Michaels repeated, pleased to have a volley partner. "So, what will it be? I've got the breadsticks, what will you bring?"

Tonya was ready for this one. "I really want to be a good teacher, so I'll bring my desire to learn." She lowered her eyebrows and frowned in thoughtfulness. "I will bring my questions and ideas to put on the table. And I will bring what I have thought about and prepared."

"Then we agree." Michaels pronounced. He had dropped what had apparently been his idea of an introductory interview and made clear his decision to accept Tonya as his independent student. "Meeting together will be a commitment we both make," he said. "It will be the same with your students. You provide the bread, the syllabus, and the textbook. They won't starve, but they'll get pretty bored. Then you will invite them to contribute. A diet of you all the time could get pretty stale, don't you think?"

Tonya loved conversational exchanges and leapt at any invitation to offer her experiences and ideas. "I've known teachers like that— one-man shows—and it got old real fast. It can be so tiring taking it in all the time without a chance to interact." She had picked up on Michaels' assumption of ongoing meetings, but she didn't want to interrupt the flow of his thinking to acknowledge his offer.

"A good teacher, Ms. Simmons, wants the interaction—and the students want it too." The chair had become too confining and Michaels began pacing behind his desk. "They want a full banquet," he went on, "not just the bread. Of course the teacher also gets tired of just bread and wants to add his or her contributions—enthusiasm, caring, challenges!" Michaels was gaining energy every minute. "A good teacher encourages interaction. Everyone gets involved. Everybody brings something to the table, and everyone goes away satisfied."

As if to punctuate his point, Dr. Michaels tapped a breadstick on the desk. "So you get what I'm saying? One-on-one or with a class of 40, learning comes from interaction. It is not one sided."

Tonya had been eying the breadsticks and couldn't restrain herself another minute. "Could I please, would you mind if I had one of those breadsticks? Talking about bread and banquets has made me really hungry."

"Be my guest, Ms. Simmons. A prop can always help you remember a point."

A self-conscious silence settled on the office–classroom as Tonya broke off pieces of the breadstick and tried to chew as quietly as possible. Dr. Michaels took the opportunity to lengthen his paces, coming to rest in front of the whiteboard that covered the west wall of his office. After what he felt was an ample amount of time for Tonya to have finished the breadstick, he launched into a new topic.

"Have you though about the impact you will make as a teacher, Ms. Simmons? Have you considered the effect you will have on your students—and the impression they will take away with them when they leave your classroom?

Tonya brushed crumbs from her lap and reached in her backpack for her water bottle, then put it back. She didn't want to be rude, and she wasn't sure what rules went with drinking from water bottles in a professor's office while he was talking. The sudden shift took her by surprise, but she had no problem with a response. "I think about it all the time," she answered. "I want them to think I am a good teacher. I want to make a positive impact on their lives."

"Try some math, Ms. Simmons." Michaels picked up a marker and twirled it between his fingers. "That okay with you?"

"Sure. I'm a math teacher—and Spanish."

"How many students do you, or will you, have in your classes every day?"

"Probably 120–125. I'll have five classes."

"And each of those students will decide if you are a good teacher or if you 'suck', to use the current vernacular. And they will tell their friends. If each student tells three friends that you are a good teacher, how many people will you have impressed?

"Could be up to 375." Tonya was quick, but it wasn't the first time she had done this exercise. The facts always impressed, if not intimidated, her.

"And then add their parents and siblings and soccer coaches and church leaders and. . . ." Dr. Michaels encouraged Tonya to interrupt with a "you go ahead" gesture.

"Lots of people would hear if I was a good teacher or if I sucked." Tonya took a breath before challenging the professor. "But so what? I want to impact them with the excitement of algebra or the value of knowing how to talk to someone who speaks another language. I don't want to be popular just because I'm nice or funny or something. I want to be a teacher who makes a difference, who changes someone's life!" For a moment she seemed surprised that she had been so confrontational, but she recovered. "I would prefer to imagine my students telling all those people about what they had learned or an idea they had discovered. Just saying I was a good teacher doesn't really mean much, don't you think?" Tonya rested her case.

"I like your emphasis," the professor conceded. "The math works the same way. You have an impact on 25 students in your Spanish class and make them love discovering how to communicate in another language. They tell three friends, and you've had an impact on 75 people with the fun and value of learning Spanish. Being thought of as 'good' and making a positive impact are pretty much the same thing. The students go home and tell parents, siblings, coaches, and you have brought a positive message to hundreds of people! That's the impact you have as a teacher. Hundreds of people. When you get a student excited about learning, hundreds of people get a positive message about teachers—and what they teach. Other students get the message and want to sign up for your classes. When you're bad—well, you know what happens then. Students avoid a bad teacher's classes, maybe even what the bad teacher teaches!"

"A bad psychology teacher means empty classes." Tonya thought about extending her example but didn't. Instead she put her backpack aside and stood in front of her chair. "I can still remember the good teachers who had a impact on me, and it's been years since, say, ninth-grade science. I must have told 50 people over the years about the day Mrs. Tice brought the poor dead skunk she had found at the side of the road into our first-period biology class. She made her (she had been pregnant) our impromptu lesson in anatomy, and we watched so intently none of us left when the bell rang." She was excited remembering, and her voice carried the energy. "Then there was Mr. Scott who read aloud the biography of Malcolm X. He read it with a passion I had never seen anyone have for history—he impressed me. I said something about him in my pre-algebra class just today! About the way he paced and gestured and held us totally captive."

Dr. Michaels stood still, twisting the pen in his hand, giving Tonya time to absorb the lesson they had worked out together. "So you understand," he said, breaking the silence, "the impact you will have—now and in the future—when you are a good teacher."

The professor shook back the sleeve of his brown sport jacket and checked his watch for the time. "We've talked about the mutual responsibility of the teacher and the students to bring something to the table. And we have seen the impact a good teacher can have on her students. Now, Ms. Simmons, the big question. Why do you want to be a teacher?"

"I have thought about that, of course. They ask you in all the interviews." Tonya bent over to grab her backpack and began to unzip the front pocket. "Actually, I have my essay response to an application question right here."

Dr. Michaels took the folded sheet and scanned the essay. "You say you want to make a difference in student's lives. You talk about being a camp counselor and how you saw the difference a good counselor made in the girl's experience at camp. You don't say so directly, but I would guess you want to save the world."

Tonya frowned and straightened her shoulders. "What's wrong with that?"

"Nothing is wrong with saving the world if you know all the problems and have all the answers, but we are talking about what you will do as a teacher. You want to make a difference in students' lives. For the better, I assume."

"Of course. I want them to care about their world so they can do something about it. To make changes they have to know more about it and how the world works. I want them to care about themselves and know that they can make a difference—that they can contribute to the life around them and make it better." Tonya felt herself bristling but made a great effort to control her tone.

"Ah! Ms. Simmons," Dr. Michaels met her defensiveness with a positive interpretation of her intentions. "You are beginning to focus in on your motive, your true motivation for becoming a teacher—a good teacher." He paused to consider his next comment. "You may not sound very original to me or to yourself. What matters is how seriously you take your mission, how you relate what you do every day to your vision."

Tonya left her chair and stood at the corner of Dr. Michaels' desk. Her voice was tight, and she made an effort to maintain her cool. "I may not be original, but I am sincere."

"The most important first step in becoming a good teacher, Ms. Simmons, is to know what you want to accomplish by being a teacher. You have made a good start, albeit rather grandiose and idealistic. Now you must examine your motives, thoughtfully. You must know what sort of a difference you want to make—and how you plan to accomplish your intention. You cannot go into the classroom on the wings of passion and good intentions but without a focus."

"How much more do I need to know beyond that I want to make a difference and be a good teacher?" Tonya was calmer, her question less a challenge than a sincere inquiry.

Noting that Tonya has dropped her guard and become more receptive, Dr. Michaels tuned it down a notch himself and spoke in a controlled, professorial voice. "You need a clear vision—a picture of what you want to give your students. Your vision is of the ideal. It is an image of what you want to accomplish as a teacher. Your mission is to bring about the vision. And as with every mission, getting to your vision takes work and time." He leaned against the whiteboard and waited a few seconds for his message to sink in. "Having the vision gives you the focus. It informs everything you do. Fulfilling the mission is your process, the process of becoming a good teacher." He paused again. "And the process never ends because part of the vision is that learning and growth never end." Michaels fanned his fingers and brought his hands to his desk with a muffled slap. His face had become pink, and his eyes gleamed.

The passion in Dr. Michaels' voice caused Tonya to turn toward him. He seemed aware that he was getting excited and paused to collect himself before going on. "First you need a vision. Then you need a mission statement that you can write down and return to frequently to test whether what you are doing is consistent with what you intend to accomplish. You need a personal mission statement that is specific enough for you to use as a touchstone, a reality check."

He folded his arms, then raised his right hand as if to write in the air. "For example," he took a step back from the desk, "a history teacher might have as part of his mission to increase his students' world awareness. How would he know if he's accomplishing this?"

Tonya, always the alert student, began to answer, and then realized the question was a rhetorical device and waited for him to go on. "Maybe he sees his students reading a newspaper. Perhaps they want to talk about a world event they saw covered on television. Could be they suggest having a current events session once a week. They're bringing questions and ideas to the table and at the same time giving evidence that the teacher is accomplishing his mission." The professor shrugged before finishing his speech. "But you won't always know how close you are to accomplishing your vision or completing your mission. Sometimes you will never know. Other times you may have to wait 10 or more years to hear from a former student that indeed your teaching did make the difference. You just have to keep your vision in sight and keep up with the process."

Dr. Michaels moved over to the bookcase and leaned back on his left shoulder. "I suggest you keep a copy of your mission statement with you, in your daybook or your wallet, as a reality check—and refer to it often. It will help you get a grip on those days when you wonder, why am I dong this? It will direct you when you aren't sure where you're going."

"I have thought about my motives and my mission. Every preparing teacher does." Standing had become awkward, and Tonya sat down again. "But I can think some more." She studied the back of her hand while gathering thoughts for her response. She began to speak, slowly and purposefully, as if discovering her ideas as she heard herself think. "Already I'm realizing," she said, "that I need to think more about how my mission will affect how I approach teaching. I need to understand how I will know whether I am accomplishing my mission. I guess my mission will be like my goals. My objectives will be what I do as a teacher to achieve those goals."

"Yes, Ms. Simmons." Dr. Michaels again looked at his watch and ran his hand through what was once mildly curly brown hair but was now somewhat flat and streaked with gray. He continued, "This is serious business, and I am serious about teaching. And so, I gather, are you." He moved toward the desk, discovered he had a pen in his hand, and returned it to the whiteboard. Back at the desk, he snapped his briefcase closed and moved toward the door. Tonya stood and swung her backpack over her left shoulder. She shuffled her feet but didn't move toward the door.

"Thank you, Dr. Michaels. You have really got me thinking. The interesting thing is, I am thinking, but what I really want to do is to get back to the classroom and teach—to do what I am thinking about."

"You strike me as sincere and willing to explore. There's a lot more to this game than having a mission." The sunlight outside the office window was fading, and the professor switched on the light. "I am willing to continue our conversation if you are willing to be prepared. And for next week, that means a vision and a mission statement—your mission statement."

"Wonderful. Thank you." Tonya sounded relieved. "I really appreciate this. And I will have the statement. Is the same time okay with you?"

Dr. Michaels collected the left over breadsticks and put them back in the drawer. "This works for me. A good start to the weekend. See you next Friday. And you will be on time."

Tonya nodded her head, still embarrassed about being late. "Yes, and I will be here on time," she said, hoping she projected both respect and gratitude.

Conversation Points

1. What is the importance of a mission statement?

2. Identify your mission and vision statement for teaching.

3. What will you do as a beginning teacher to encourage your students to "bring something to the table"?

CONVERSATION TWO

Expectations

Our circumstances answer to our expectations and the demand of our natures.

—Henry David Thoreau

Tonya couldn't shake the mission challenge Dr. Michaels had tossed at her. Friday night, after her meeting with the revered professor, she and her boyfriend, Jason, a graduate student in chemistry, ordered pizza and made jabbing attempts at picking up a week's worth of accumulated papers, books, and shoes to make the apartment presentable for the weekend. All evening, Tonya talked about her meeting with Dr. Michaels and what she intended to accomplish as a teacher. *Intended* seemed a better word than *hoped* or *wanted*—more active and committed. She probed and dissected Jason's memories of teachers and professors who had influenced him and left a lasting impression. She reviewed her own experiences, wondering if what had impressed her about great teachers she had known had anything to do with their missions or motives. By Saturday morning, she had concluded that her mission statement, what she wanted and intended to achieve as a great teacher, was her personal guide and goal. The impression she left with her students would reflect her having achieved her goals rather than reveal her tenets.

She had also realized that she wanted to be a great teacher. A good teacher is competent. She wanted to be more than competent, better than good. *Excellent* seemed like a higher degree of good, an

A rather than an A–. *Great*, Tonya concluded, transcended *excellent*. Great went beyond the classroom. Great extended into the future. She planned to be a great teacher who made a difference in how her students approached, appreciated, and lived their lives.

On Sunday, Jason went to the lab, and Tonya gave her full attention to her lessons for the next week and to a paper she had for her foreign language methods class. On and off during the week, she jotted notes for the mission statement she had promised to prepare for her Friday meeting with Dr. Michaels. Thursday night, she typed out her thoughts, titling her draft, "Mission in Process."

Friday afternoon, she went through the door on the third floor of the education building fifteen minutes early, feeling the excitement of being prepared and looking forward to what she and the professor would discuss. In her backpack, she had two apples and a wedge of brie cheese—her symbol for what she was bringing to the table.

Sensing it would be just as wrong to be early as late, Tonya waited out the fifteen minutes by reading the bulleting board ads for study-abroad programs and summer workshops.

At four o'clock, she knocked on the professor's door.

"Hello Ms. Simmons," he greeted her welcomingly. "You come with a mission!"

She acknowledged his humor with a smile and handed him the printout of her draft. As he was reading, she put the brie and apples on the desk next to the breadsticks.

"Ah," he said, "we shall feast today!"

"Well?" Tonya presented the question as Dr. Michaels gestured for her to take the chair across from him.

"You've been thinking, Tonya. You are using language that takes responsibility for acting on your motives. You write, 'I will share with my students my commitment to and passion for language study as a means to knowing other peoples and other cultures. I will do this as a means to encourage and direct their enthusiasm for language learning and global awareness.' Thanks for the brie, and thank you also for challenging me to again think about my motives—what they were when I was a high school government teacher and what they became when I earned my doctorate and came to teach preservice teachers at this university."

Dr. Michaels pulled open the same file drawer that had yielded the breadsticks and produced paper plates, a roll of paper towels, and a wooden-handled knife. He passed the knife to Tonya, who cut the apples and opened the wrapping on the cheese.

"Why do you call this a mission in process?" Dr. Michaels handed the paper back to Tonya, took up a breadstick and cut a piece of cheese.

"Because even as I was working on my mission, it kept changing. Each day after school, I would review my experiences and the new potentials I discovered by being in the classroom. I realized how much I had yet to discover and learn about being a teacher. My mission today is based on what I have experienced and know right now, but I know that will expand. I don't want a mission statement that limits me. I don't want to set fixed goals before I see more of the possibilities."

"I understand what you're saying. My mission, my motives, have changed, especially over that past 10 years. It's time I revisit those old thoughts and bring them in line with what I'm doing today. How can I know if I'm there if I haven't any idea of where I want to be? But, as they say, enough about me."

"Even though I don't have a mission statement I am ready to have engraved on a plaque," Tonya added, her voice sounding confident, "I'm glad that I went through the exercise. I have something to come back to, to check in with and revise to keep myself on track and to keep me motivated."

"Right. And as we've heard before in a variety of contexts, much of the value in working out a mission statement is in the process. The product, by the definition we have given it, is a protean thing."

Dr. Michaels grabbed a piece of apple as he stood up and walked to the whiteboard. With pen in hand, he turned to face Tonya as he might position himself to address a class of 50 students. "So," he began in a professorial voice, "I have another challenge for you. You have investigated your motives, now consider your expectations." As he drew out his annunciation of *expectations*, he wrote the word at the top of the board in four-inch-high red letters.

"But," Tonya responded with a hint of defensiveness, "aren't my motives what I expect to accomplish? How are motives and expectations different?"

"Think of buying a car. You know what a car is supposed to do, and you want a car that will deliver. You have expectations for the car." He stopped talking and looked at Tonya, waiting for her to pick up on the idea.

"Okay. I expect the car to operate properly, to run well. I expect the brakes will work and the lights will go on and that it won't break down in the parking lot after the library has closed. But what does that have to do with teaching?"

"Before you could expect those things of the car, you had to do some investigating. You learned what to expect by learning facts about the car's history, if it's a used car. You may have studied consumer reports for ratings on what to expect of the car's performance. You didn't go into the situation blind. You had expectations, and you have expectations for yourself as a teacher."

"Yes, but I'm still a bit lost here." Tonya looked perplexed but involved in where the discussion was going.

"As a teacher," Dr. Michaels said, looking at the pen in his hand as if afraid it would jump for the board and begin writing without him, "you have expectations for yourself. And, as in buying a car, one of those expectations—I assume—is that you will prepare, that you will be prepared." That said, he wrote "PREPARED" on the board and seemed for the moment satisfied that he had made his point.

"What other expectations do you have for yourself as a teacher, Ms. Simmons? Don't be limited by the car example. Let your mind go—your ideas flow." He smiled at his impromptu rhyme, more embarrassed than proud. Tonya acknowledged his awkwardness with a brief smile, and then began thinking out loud, as was her style.

"I expect to be prepared in my subject matter. I also expect to be prepared to manage the classroom. I expect to know the rules of the school. I expect to listen to my students and to learn who they are and what they care about."

The professor added her ideas to the board and encouraged her to continue. "I guess I also expect that I will have some bad days, lessons that don't work, discipline issues—that sort of thing." Tonya waited a few seconds before adding, "And I expect that I will confront what went wrong and learn from mistakes that I expect I will make—even if I try not to."

"So you do have expectations for yourself, and reasonable ones. As you go along your expectations for yourself will grow with experience. But let's go on to other expectations that play into the total climate of your classroom." Michaels capped the red pen with a snap and picked up a green one. "What about expectations for your students? Your expectation for your students anticipates the climate, as I said, of your classroom." He wrote "EXPECTATIONS" on the left side of the board in green and in parenthesis under the word printed "for students." Realizing he was on a roll, Tonya didn't interject her next thought but waited for the professor to finish his point.

"For example," he continued, "I have expectations for you. Our situation is different from a classroom. This isn't a formal class, but we are both giving time to the project. I have expectations for what you will bring to the table. So far you are meeting those expectations—and I don't mean the cheese and apple, though I thank you for that contribution, too. You are bringing your enthusiasm and your ideas and your interest and your questions."

"And that is what I will expect of my students." Tonya was aware of interjecting, but the energy of the conversation invited her to jump into the exchange. "I will expect them to participate. I expect to have an interactive classroom where we all, to use your phrase, bring something to the table—the sort of preparation and attitudes we have been talking about."

Dr. Michaels was pacing now, snapping the lid on his pen, thinking ahead of himself but putting a check on his momentum. He again switched pens, this time choosing the blue one. "So, Ms. Simmons, you have expectations for yourself, and you have expectations for your students. What's missing?"

"Students have expectations for me—and for themselves," Tonya answered a bit bored with the obvious but polite enough not to convey that thought to the professor.

"You bet," he said with enthusiasm. "At the beginning of this semester, I asked my preservice seminar students what were their expectations for this class. I got blank stares, though I am sure they had ideas churning in the depths. Experience had taught them to expect to sit there and absorb what I had to say. They expected to sit, take in information, and regurgitate that information on quizzes and a final exam." The good professor was getting steamed. He put the pen back in the trough and leaned toward Tonya, splaying his fingers on the desk. "If they weren't going to be honest and tell me their expectations, I was certainly going to tell them mine. I told them what I expected of myself, similar to what we have up here." He gestured to the board, stopping with a puzzled look to realize he hadn't written down all the ideas they had generated. "Then I told them what I expected of them—that they would contribute and participate, that they would not be warm-bodied tape recorders but active, involved, contributing participants. I told them I had high expectations for what we could learn together, a result that we could never achieve if I did all the work and they sat passively sopping up what I shoveled out."

"I like that, Dr. Michaels. And what you do is consistent with what you expect. You expect me to be at the table and, in turn, I expect it of myself. That is what I want to accomplish with my students. I want them to expect to contribute and to participate—and to be prepared.

We have learned as preservice teachers the effect of expectation on students' performance. But expectation goes beyond just 'expecting' our students to do well on tests. I should begin by expecting—and engendering—an attitude in my students, the attitude that they are part of the process and that their contributions will enhance their learning. Then, I hope, they will come to expect more of themselves as participants in the learning process." Tonya felt her cheeks getting warm as she grew excited about the ideas she and Dr. Michaels had generated.

"One more expectation, Ms. Simmons, that I want you to consider before we end this afternoon. I want you to think about your expectations for caring about your students—and the expectations your students have for you caring about them." The professor's tone had become serious as he placed the concept of caring on the table. "It looks as if we have a series of lessons going here." He put his hands in his jacket pockets and smiled at Tonya, who hadn't yet reached to pick up her backpack. "Last time we talked about having a motive for teaching, writing out your own mission statement. Today we have talked about expectations you have as a teacher and expectations your students have for you. Next week, we will talk about caring. If you haven't already, I suggest you become familiar with Nel Noddings's book. Here, let me lend you my copy."

As the professor searched through books on his shelf, Tonya cleaned up the brie and apples. He found the book and handed it to her, taking the opportunity to check the watch on his exposed wrist. "We're moving along. I look forward to our conversation next Friday, Ms. Simmons. Same time—and I'll still have breadsticks."

"I feel I'm getting a whole lot more than breadsticks," Tonya said as she moved toward the door.

Conversation Points

1. What general expectations do you have for your students, parents, and administrators?

2. List five expectations you have for yourself.

3. What will you do to create an environment where students begin to develop high expectations of their classroom achievement?

CONVERSATION THREE

Caring

Too often we underestimate the power of touch, a smile, a kind word, a listening ear, an honest compliment, or the smallest act of caring, all of which have the potential to turn a life around.

—Leo Buscaglia

Dr. Michaels got to his office later than he had planned. The discussions with Tonya had left him curiously elated—excited—impatient to meet with his seminar of preservice students. He also felt irritable, less in control of the hour-to-hour predictable life he had arranged for his sunset years. What had his motives been 28 years ago when he chose to become a teacher? What had he expected of himself and of the high school students who shoved and shuffled into his first period class? He couldn't return to that pure state of beginning. He tried to recreate those early days, but he couldn't get back to the impetus that had propelled him to spend hours preparing lessons, listening to students, and attending their concerts and games. It concerned him that he had become competent, that he had lost his ability to be great. "Maybe I'm just getting old," he thought. Once he had wanted to engage and inspire those young people to love what he loved and to grow as they learned. That was it: He had cared. He had cared enormously about those boys and girls in his classroom and how he as a teacher would affect their lives. The responsibility he had felt came close to paralyzing him if he thought too much about it, and he did think about it—all the time. But the caring and the responsibility were also exciting and wonderful and brought forth an energy that on the best days transformed him from a competent, good teacher to a great teacher!

He was late getting back to the third floor because he had experienced a resurgence of that caring and energy in the seminar that afternoon. It had started, he realized, with Tonya and her sincerity in wanting to be a good teacher. He cared about her concerns and determination and began to see that the young men and women in his class wanted to be good teachers, too. And if they weren't as driven and passionate as Tonya, maybe he could inspire them to be. The students had responded with an openness and enthusiasm of their own. A few who had free time had stayed after the class, continuing an idea, asking questions, sharing some of their experiences. Michaels had felt his adrenalin pumping, and he was still high as he unlocked his office door and cleared a place on his desk in preparation for his hour with Tonya.

Right on time, Tonya appeared at the open door and presented the professor with two oversized chocolate chip cookies. "My contribution for the day," she said as a greeting.

"I've been reading the book you lent me, about caring, and I got so excited, I couldn't wait to talk with you about Noddings's ideas."

Michaels needed to come down from his high, or at least channel his bursting energy, before he got carried away with enthusiasm and lost control of the meeting. "Before we do a book review here, Ms. Simmons," he said with a mild sarcastic air, trying to lead her into a more thoughtful, less emotive mode, "tell me what you have gained so far from our conversations. You came in three weeks ago saying you wanted to be a good teacher. What are you thinking about that now?"

"I am more determined than ever that teaching is what I want to do. The more I think about my motives, the kind of difference I want to make, the better I believe I can understand my expectations and make it happen. But I can't be a teacher without students to teach. We talk, and you give me challenges and ideas, and I get excited but it doesn't go anywhere until I can be with my students and make it happen." Tonya had not yet taken her customary seat. Neither had the professor, who found he was grabbing for a pen and writing "CARING" in huge, green letters.

"Your mission is to make a difference, and your expectations are to care!" Dr. Michaels seemed pleased with himself at having created a coherent segue into the promised topic for the day. "I have another article for you." The professor hoisted his brief case onto the desk and zipped open the top. "Hang on . . . here it is." He handed Tonya a single sheet of printed copy. His smile suggested a pleased-with-himself pride at having found just the right reference for the day's topic.

Too impatient to wait for Tonya to read the article for herself, Michaels jumped in. "This guy Richard Traina is president of Clark University. He wanted to know what made a good teacher. He did some research. He looked at autobiographies of 125 prominent Americans from the 19th and 20th centuries to see what they had to say about teachers they valued. He discovered an extraordinary, consistent pattern in what they described as a good teacher, or good and memorable teacher." After a spin around his desk and a pause to look out the window, he was back at the whiteboard and poised to write, this time with his black pen. "The three characteristics described time and time again by these Americans were. . . ." He wrote as he talked. "Factor One was, not surprisingly, competence in the subject matter. The second factor identified in the autobiographies was caring deeply about students and their success, and the third factor was a distinctive character." The three factors were listed in a row, numbered 1, 2, and 3. "Right now let's keep our attention on one and two, caring mainly." He sounded to Tonya as if he were addressing a class, although she was the only other person in the room. Once a teacher, always a teacher, she thought to herself and smiled.

"Character is a subject for another session," he continued to lecture, "although certainly a caring teacher demonstrates a distinctive character. Caring, in my experience, comes first—then, because a genuinely caring teacher loses his or her ego in reaching out to the students, the individual character reveals itself. A great teacher, Tonya, is a teacher who cares—and who acts on that caring."

Tonya was aching to get into the conversation. "Yes, I can believe that about the importance of caring in making a good—a great—teacher! The teachers I remember, who had an impact on me, all really cared! They were all good with their subjects, and I respected them for what they knew, but I responded to them because they let me—and the other students—know they cared."

"Consider this, Tonya," Dr. Michaels said, directing her attention to the board as he wrote, in solid purple ink and great block letters. "Students not only care what you know, but they want to know that you care." He stepped back so she could take in the meaning of his epigram. "Yes," he said, looking directly at Tonya, back to having a one-on-one conversation. "Students need to respect your command of the subject matter. They want you to be at ease with your subject and excited about what you've learned and know. They want you not to be a history teacher, but a teacher of history! That gives them confidence in you. But also—and equally important—they want to know that you care about them. That lets them open up to you so you can learn together." He let a silence drop as if he were punctuating the end of an important speech.

When Tonya, who was frozen in a moment of prolonged thoughtfulness, didn't break into the silence, Michaels interrupted her reverie with a question. "Okay, Tonya," he began in a teacherly voice, "You want to be good. You already care about that. How will you know that you care about your students? How will your students know that you care about them?"

"With the students in my practice teaching section, I know I care," Tonya answered right away with solid assurance. "I want them to succeed. I care about what they accomplish and how they grow. I know because I feel it. It goes back to wanting to make a difference. The students—how they feel, how they learn—it matters to me!" Tonya, now moving around the office in Dr. Michaels's wake, drew her hands into fists and beat them against her thighs. "I care!"

"I believe you do, Tonya," Dr. Michaels interjected, using his professor voice to calm her intensity. "And how," he asked again, "will your students know you care?"

"Because of what I do, I guess. I will have to think about what my memorable teachers did to make me know they cared. Again, my good teachers are still my teachers!"

"Going back to Traina's article," the professor said, picking up his copy of the page he had given Tonya, "when Traina looked at what the people in his study said about their caring teachers, here is what he concluded." His orator's voice captured Tonya's attention. "It began," he read, quoting the article, "with the teacher recognizing the student as an individual who brings particular experiences, interest, enthusiasm, and fears to the classroom. It was the teacher taking time to acknowledge a student's life outside the classroom, inquiring about the family's welfare or the student's participation in an extracurricular activity. It moved to an instance that the student takes pride in his or her work—stretching each person to a level of performance that surprised and delighted the student." He put the paper on his desk and looked to Tonya for a response.

"That's it! I knew they cared because they paid attention to me. Once we had an assignment, in ninth grade I think, to write about a place we though was beautiful. I wrote about a section of the park.

The teacher, Mrs. Cherry, asked me if I would show her my place in the park. One afternoon, she met me after school, and we went to the place I had described. My friend Joan, who often went with me to the fern grove, came, too. I was so pleased that my writing had made an impression on someone. After that, I really cared about writing. I felt important. I knew that Mrs. Cherry cared."

"Your teacher was involved. You mattered. She cared." Dr. Michaels finally pulled out his chair and sat down. "When you stop caring, you stop being a great teacher."

"I can't imagine not caring. If I stopped caring, where would the energy come from?" Tonya seemed concerned, and Dr. Michaels responded to her question.

"You are right, Tonya, to connect caring and energy, and Lord knows teaching requires plenty of energy." He stretched his arms and let them fall back to the armrests on his chair. "I realized how essential caring is to good teaching when I lost my focus and my energy became a sham. I had been teaching maybe 10 or 12 years. I was married then, and tensions at home were draining my energy and diverting my focus. I couldn't give the caring my students deserved because I was so caught up in my own problems. Maybe I was on the edge of burnout after a decade in the classroom; I'm not sure of all the causes. The point is, I knew I wasn't giving the students all that I had in the past, all that I knew I wanted to give to be a good teacher. They sensed it, too. We went along by rote and kept our polite distance. I was dry and empty and angry—spent."

"So what did you do?"

"I left the front of the classroom and took a seat facing the teacher. I went back to school to finish my PhD. I was still involved in education, but as an observer and not as a teacher. I didn't really have a mission, other than to be doing something related to what had been my chosen field." Michaels turned his hands palms up as if asking for understanding.

"But you got it back, didn't you? You're teaching now—do you care like you did before?" Tonya leaned forward in her chair, pleading for a reassuring answer.

"I am asking more of my students. When they care, I can't help but respond. Then I get involved and interested and excited about what we're doing and learning together. Some days, I feel like a teacher again—because on those days I care."

Dr. Michaels looked as if he wanted to say more, but instead he shifted the subject to Noddings's book. "So, did you have time to look over Dr. Noddings's thoughts on caring?" Tonya found the book in her stuffed backpack and extracted it with care—to show respect for the book Michaels had lent her and to make sure no candy wrappers or mangled notebook pages followed.

"To tell you the truth, I checked out the table of contents and read a bit here and there, but I can't say I could take a test on it or anything. I'd have to spend more time. She, at least in what I read, looks at caring as it applies to education in a general sense—the nature of the institution, learning, and curriculum. What she says early in the book about teachers as the carers and students as the cared-for seems to connect with what we—you—have been saying this afternoon."

"Dr. Noddings's work has had an important influence on my approach to teaching and has given me some insight on the problem, or should I say my problem, with teaching." As the professor turned away from Tonya and scanned his wall of books, Tonya began to speak, and then paused for a minute with her mouth half open, wondering if she should push the issue. She concluded that he wouldn't have opened the door if he didn't want her to enter, so she accepted the invitation and jumped.

"You have a problem with teaching? Whatever that problem is, the people I have talked with haven't noticed any. Everyone thinks you're the greatest. 'He cares' is what I hear over and over again. And that's what we're talking about, isn't it? Caring?"

Dr. Michaels picked up the book from where Tonya had placed it on his desk and began to fan through the familiar pages. With the book open in his left hand, he went to the whiteboard and pointed to the word written in large green letters. "CARING," he said, underlining the word. "Caring is relational. See, Tonya, a caring relation is, according to Noddings, in its most basic form, a connection or encounter between two human beings—a carer, as you identified earlier, and a recipient of care, or the cared-for."

"Here, let me read what she says about the caring relationship and how it applies to teaching. Okay, now, here it is. Noddings writes, 'In order for the relation to be properly called caring, both parties must contribute to it in characteristic ways. A failure on the part of either carer or cared-for blocks completion of caring and, although there may still be, in relation—that is, an encounter or connection in which each party feels something toward the other—it is not a caring relation.'" The professor stopped and looked to see if Tonya was with him. Satisfied that she was alert, he continued—almost as if he were giving a dramatic reading. "'No matter how hard teachers try to care,'" he slowed down and looked up over the page at his wholly attentive student, "'if the caring is not received by students, the claim "they don't care" has some validity. It suggests strongly that something is wrong.'"

"Going back to what we were saying earlier, Dr. Michaels, what exactly is caring, or should I say, a caring relation? How do you do it?" Tonya squared her shoulders as if prepared for combat, daring the professor or his book to have an answer.

The professor took on the challenge by continuing to read. "'Caring is not, infatuation, enchantment or obsession, but a full receptivity.'" He looked over the book to be sure Tonya was following him. Satisfied he had her full attention, he went on quoting Noddings. "'When I care, I really hear, see, or feel what the other tries to convey. [I am] seized by the needs of others.'"

Tonya was ready to push her point. "She still isn't saying what we do when we care," she came back. "She seems to be describing how we feel when we care."

"That's exactly what she says. The hearing and feeling characterize what she calls 'our consciousness when we care.' Tell me, Tonya, how can you tell if someone—a teacher, for example—cares? How can you tell if a teacher is in a state of caring consciousness?"

"Well," Tonya took a few seconds to remember past moments and teachers whom she would say had cared. "I would say it has something to do with how a teacher pays attention to you. You know if someone is really listening, is really hearing what you are saying and not just waiting to jump in with a lecture or something."

Michaels snapped the pen top, spun on his heels, and came to rest with his elbows on the desk, leaning toward Tonya. She startled but held her ground, waiting for his response.

"That's a big part of it. When you care, the listening comes naturally. Because you want to really hear. You want to know what the student is thinking." He took a breath and stood up, moving again to the board and choosing a green pen. "ARE YOU LISTENING FOR UNDERSTANDING," he wrote as he spoke, "OR SPEAKING TO BE HEARD?"

"Yes. That's it!" Tonya all but clapped her hands in agreement with the professor. "You can tell when someone is really listening and taking in what you are saying. A lot of the time, though, especially in a classroom, you feel the teacher is just waiting you out, waiting for you to finish so she can get back to what she wanted to say in the first place. That's the 'speaking to be heard' you were talking about. Real caring, real listening can be hard work, but it is so important for good teachers to listen. When a teacher truly listens, she can respond to what she heard and come much closer to meeting the student's needs for recognition—and for information that matters."

"Listening is a valuable component of caring, but note that Noddings warns us there is no easy set of steps to follow if you want to show caring. 'Caring,' she is careful to remind us, 'is a way of being in relation, not a set of specific behaviors.'" The professor took his time writing out the reminder, as if using the pause to decide where the discussion would go next. When he turned around, he had lost some of his frenetic energy and appeared almost sad.

"Caring is relation," he repeated, "between the carer and the cared-for, or you could say, the cared-about. Responses from the cared-for encourage and reward the carer, as in the case of a mother with a child. If the child doesn't respond in an encouraging and rewarding way, the caregiver can become worn out. Think, Tonya, how it might be for you when you have a classroom of students and you truly care. You listen. What they say, what they need, what you have to offer them really matters. But they don't respond."

"That would be so frustrating, and exhausting. If I had a class like that, I don't know. I am realistic, I think. I'd want to, but I am not sure I'd be able to connect in a caring way with every student. But with the class as a whole, I'd hope I could." Tonya slumped in the wooden chair as if some sustaining force had drained out of her.

"Noddings recognizes the possibility you just identified. Listen to this," Michaels picked up the book. "Teachers, too, suffer this dreadful loss of energy when their students do not respond."

"Then what happens? Is that the burnout you hear so much about? Do you stop caring when they don't reciprocate? Or can you fix it?"

"Tonya," the professor leaned back and sat on the desk, looking at his one student. "It's easy to stop caring. You're exhausted and, yes, this is burnout. Maybe you shouldn't be in the classroom if you can't care. Maybe you should take yourself away and make room for a teacher who can communicate that caring."

"But it could be just that one class, or that one situation. If a teacher really cares, she wouldn't give up—I wouldn't. I think I'd just care right through the problem, listen, and hear—until we got it back—the relation that is."

"Or until you get the response you need to know your caring is received. Yes, Tonya, caring is at the core. You want to be a great teacher, and to be a great teacher you have to care. I think you do—about being a teacher, and about your students." Dr. Michaels checked that all the pens had their caps, then opened his case and pulled out some stapled papers and gave them to Tonya. "Some articles I copied for you, and some pages from Dr. Noddings's book that you should read carefully."

"Thank you. And again, thank you for your time. I am learning so much about the teacher I want to be."

Dr. Michaels waited for her to go out first, then followed, pulling the door closed. "I'm good for next week," he offered.

"Great. May I bring some questions, some issues I've been thinking about?"

"Sounds good. See you in seven." Tonya headed for the stairs. The professor entered the department office and searched his box for messages.

Conversation Points

1. What are some strategies you can initiate to create a caring environment in your classroom?

2. How are ego and caring related?

3. What does the statement, "Students not only care what you know, but want to know you care" mean to you?

CONVERSATION FOUR

Commitment

*There are countless ways of achieving greatness, but any
road to achieving one's maximum potential must be built
on a bedrock of respect for the individual, a commitment
to excellence, and a rejection of mediocrity.*

—Buck Rodgers

Tonya waited, shifting her backpack from one shoulder to the
other, until she heard the professor sign off from his phone
conversation. With a resigned sigh, she knocked and pushed the
door open when he invited her in. Michaels looked up from chair
but didn't move except to gesture toward the empty seat. Before
she sat down, Tonya searched in her backpack for a manila envelope
she extracted and slid across the desk.

"Here's my contribution for the day," she said with unmasked
anger and frustration. "I might as well give it up now. No 'great
teacher.' Not even an 'atta girl.' I might as well quit now, give the
whole thing up today."

"Should I open this? Is it a subpoena or something?" Michaels
asked.

"Yeah, go ahead. It's my student teacher evaluation—even
though we have a week to go."

"Why don't you just tell me about it?"

"She, Mrs. Calder, seems to think I'm not organized. Maybe it
looks that way at times, but it's because I do listen, and I do hear, and
I get excited about responding to what the students are into. Yeah, so
we get off track, but I think they are learning."

"Anything else?"

"Well, she said I get too involved. I shouldn't help them so much. Stuff about leading, not solving."

"Anything good? Did she have any positive comments? Or was it a free-for-all dump-on-Tonya day?"

"I guess. She likes my energy, and she says I know my stuff and can see I care. Even if she thinks I'm not organized, at least she likes my intentions. She gave my lesson plans an A."

"Sounds good to me."

"But she gave me a B+ for the semester!"

"This is just the beginning. Now its up to you to decide how you will respond."

Tonya crossed her arms over her chest. "I have been thinking about quitting," she said. "If I can't be a really good teacher, I don't want to be a teacher at all. Some of the other student teachers, I don't know if they really care about teaching, making that impact we talked about. One guy, he just wants a job with summers off so he can bike over a mountaintop somewhere. Another woman—she's an art teacher—she just wants to make some money so she can support her painting. That's not why I'm doing this, to have a job. I am really committed to teaching—to being a good teacher. Or at least I was. Now I wonder if I should rethink the whole damn thing."

"Hey, wait a minute. You've got one of the most important foundations for being a good teacher. You just said it yourself. You are committed."

Neither Tonya nor Michaels had moved from their places during this exchange. The envelope remained on the desk. After twirling the envelope around with his index finger, Michaels leaned forward and pushed himself to his feet. He moved slowly to the board, opened a purple pen, and wrote COMMITMENT in capital letters.

"So, this is our conversation on commitment," Tonya said, acknowledging the message. "Part of me wants to quit. Why make the effort if I won't ever been any good? Another part of me wants to fight back and get better."

"Go back to—what was it? Our second conversation? Go back to your mission statement. Your motive." The professor waited.

"That I want to make a difference. All that about wanting students to learn and to enhance their lives. And my expectations for how that could happen, the expectations for myself and for them. And caring—that what happens with learning is something that really matters to me." Tonya slumped in the wooden chair. She looked defeated and stormy, as if crying would be a relief.

Michaels gave her a moment to herself, then, without saying a thing, pointed to the purple word on the white board.

"I guess I am committed. Teaching is what I have always wanted. It isn't a means to something else for me—like biking around the world or selling an oil painting for five thousand dollars. A teacher. That's who I want to be."

Dr. Michaels watched with interest as Tonya seemed to detach from the moment, her gaze drifting, and her eyebrows moving closer together in a thoughtful scowl. After a few seconds she came back with an excited smile. "I was remembering a bit from Pat Conroy's *The Prince of Tides,*" she explained to the professor. "I read the book in high school, and what he said about being a teacher really struck me. It still leaves me with a shiver when I remember." She took a breath and gathered herself together. "Tom, the guy who is telling the story, is talking to his twin sister. She says he has sold himself short, that he could have been more than a teacher and a coach. He explains himself, saying, 'There's no word in the language I revere more than teacher. None. My heart sings when a kid refers to me as his teacher and it always has. I've honored myself and the entire family of man by becoming one.'"

Both Michaels and Tonya were silent for a few seconds. The professor nodded in recognition and went over to his bookshelf. He pulled an old paperback from the shelf and opened it so Tonya could see the dog-eared page. He replaced the book and returned to his desk and the manila envelope.

"And the evaluation," Dr. Michaels broke the silence and handed the envelope back to Tonya. "What will you do about that—not that it's such a horrible thing?"

"In my good moments," Tonya said, smiling slightly, "I realize Mrs. Calder is a teacher—and a good one—and I am the student. She wants me to learn, and I want to. I know what she means about getting off track. I think my motives are right, but maybe I need to work on my technique? Even though I want the students to be involved and I want to listen and follow their thoughts, I need to stay in control of where we are going. Isn't that, after all, what they expect of me? To have a plan of where I want them to go—what I hope they will learn?"

"Sometimes they won't even know you are leading. A good teacher will often let the students think they found the way themselves. But you are right. They expect you to be in charge—and they respect you for it."

"And the other thing goes along with being involved and in charge and all that. I do get excited, I admit that. When I see a student reaching, I want to help. But I shouldn't do too much, or they will never know the real fun and satisfaction of discovering for themselves. She's right."

"So you aren't quitting? You'll hang in there and finish the semester and show up next fall to meet your new students?"

"Yes, of course. I knew all along, but I was just so discouraged when I got the evaluation. But I am committed."

The phone rang. Dr. Michaels indicated to Tonya that he had to take the call. She opened her notebook and jotted some thoughts as he talked to the person on the line. When he hung up, she asked her question.

"Why does it make me so mad to hear that guy talk about his summers off or to hear Jana go on about her painting? That doesn't make them bad people, I guess. It's just that I want them to do it my way. I want all teachers to be committed to their students first. The other stuff can come later. Their job is teaching. I take it personally when they aren't as committed as I am!"

"We get to it different ways, Tonya," Michaels responded. "Sometimes we have to discover the commitment. I'll tell you a story."

The professor wandered over and sat on the desk, turning the pen in his hand. "When I first started teaching, I wanted to change the world. Sound familiar? I was interested in political issues, and I wanted to be where it was happening. So I got involved. In delegations, with candidates, that sort of thing. I had my teaching job and I had my commitment to changing the world. But it was spreading me thin. This is too much, I thought. I can't have my head in Washington and my job in Illinois. So I focused my energies on more local issues and got really involved. Worked late at night and weekends on local issues. And I lectured my students on the importance of commitment. They listened, but my issues weren't their issues. That caring thing. I wasn't caring enough about them to really hear their issues or what they wanted to learn. I taught the curriculum and went to meetings at the city council after school. Then I read their evaluations. Yes, they got to write up evaluations of their teachers. They didn't think I cared. Caring—commitment. From the students' perspective, the two go together."

"So, what happened? Did you do something?"

"With the help of my administrator, yes. He challenged me that I couldn't have two commitments at once. He asked directly if I was committed to teaching, or did I want to run for office. Then he put it straight. What really mattered?"

"Back to the mission thing, right?"

"Yes, I guess. I spent a long weekend looking at what I imagine you could call my mission. I concluded that I wanted, like you, to make a difference. And finally I came to realize that I could best make that difference in the classroom with my students. I saw my commitment to teaching as a commitment to the people who would shape our world tomorrow. And I went back to the classroom with a renewed commitment to those kids and to teaching. I became present for them and committed to being a good teacher for them."

"And from what people remember, you were—a great teacher."

"Well, thanks, Tonya. Yes, for a while I was a completely committed, caring teacher. That's what students deserve and what they should expect. It's an honor to be a teacher—and it isn't easy."

"No. And getting discouraged is, I guess, to be expected. That evaluation punched me in the gut, but I can learn from what she said. Anyway, I'm back. And more aware than ever of all I want to think about before next fall. I'm committed, and I want to be as prepared as possible." Tonya began packing up, starting with the manila envelope she lifted from Professor Michaels's desk. "So what's next? Do I have an assignment for next week, Professor?"

"Focus on your commitment. You've got one week to go as a preservice teacher. Think about what you've learned and who you want to be—for your students. Finish up the semester in a burst of glory—have fun."

"Sounds like a bit much, but I'll give it my best. Thanks. See you next week."

Tonya closed the door behind her and stood quietly for a moment before heading for the stairs.

Conversation Points

1. Identify your level of commitment to the teaching profession.

2. How will your commitment separate you from the rest of your colleagues?

3. How will you get your students to bring a high level of commitment to your classroom?

CONVERSATION FIVE

Respect

> *Treat people as if they were what they ought to be and you help them to become what they are capable of being.*
>
> —Johann Wolfgang von Goethe

Tonya and Dr. Michaels approached each other from opposite ends of the hall. From a distance she could see he had a serious but relaxed look. He could tell that Tonya was upbeat and flushed with excited energy.

"Today I brought you something I got yesterday from one of my students," Tonya began before the professor had gotten his briefcase open or the lights turned on. "I had to show someone, and I thought you would understand." She handed over a card and a folded piece of notepaper. "Read it and give me your reaction—please."

Michaels opened the notepaper and read out loud, "Thank you, Miss Simmons. You taught us a lot. You listened and you cared about us. I wasn't your best student, but you never made me feel stupid— and I even like math now. You'll be a great teacher.' " The professor slowly refolded the note and looked at Tonya. "So, what do you think, Ms. Simmons?"

"It makes me feel so good, like it's all worth it, like maybe I am making a difference." She hesitated, and then asked, "Am I overreacting?"

Michaels disregarded her question, waiting for Tonya to lead the way. "I have two more," she said, offering them to the professor.

When he didn't reach for the notes, Tonya looked confused. "Why don't you read them to me?" he asked, phrasing his plea as a mild challenge.

"I don't know. It's kind of embarrassing I guess, but okay." Tonya looked at Michaels and then at the notes. "This one says, 'It must be hard to be a student teacher, but you didn't do bad. I liked that you could laugh even when it was an important lesson. Thank you, Zach Taylor.' And this one is from a girl in the Spanish class who was always shy about talking and turned all splotchy if she thought she had to read something out loud. She gave me this card—the card is a thank you in Spanish, but she wrote, in English, 'You are a very good teacher. You paid attention to us and you respected us. Have fun being a teacher. The kids who get you are lucky.' That's it. What do you think?"

"Again, Tonya, you tell me what you think."

"Well, they say some of the things we have talked about. They mentioned that I listened and that I cared and that I could laugh. It's good, isn't it, that they noticed—and that they wrote the notes? Or do you want me to worry about what all the other students were thinking. Do you think I should be discouraged because I got only three notes—though a bunch of the kids did come up to say thank you and good luck?"

"Not at all, Tonya. The notes are great. Save them. Create a 'feel good' file. They will remind you why you're a teacher. And don't assume that the silent ones didn't appreciate your teaching. Often years will go by before you know what kind of impact you had on a student. In fact, last Saturday at the supermarket someone I recognized but couldn't immediately place came up to me. I flashed on her name the minute she said, 'Mr. Michaels'!

"'Hello, Christy!' I said, feeling proud of myself. 'How have you been?'

"She answered that she had been fine and had often thought of the class she had with me her junior year. She used some of the same words your students did. She said I had been the first teacher she really respected, that I had heard what the students had to say and that I had honestly cared. Then her husband came up, and she introduced me as 'that great teacher I always talk about.' Christy has kids in high school today. That's a long time to wait for feedback, but I appreciate it never the less. The impression we make lasts a lifetime in some cases—and in most cases we will never know."

"Makes me realize that I never said thank you to some of the teachers who have affected my life," Tonya said. "And it also makes me realize that it isn't too late. What is the lesson here, Professor? I know, you're going to ask me what I think is the lesson. Well, I guess to be true to my motives and commitment and to believe in myself and in my students."

"You're getting it, Ms. Simmons. But before you put those notes away, I want to call your attention to what I believe is one of the central concepts all good teachers must embrace and express. Respect. Your student said she respected you. Your students knew you respected them because you listened and you demonstrated caring."

Dr. Michaels had gone a full ten minutes without writing on his board, perhaps a record! But the temptation—or the impulse—got the better of him, and he pushed away from his desk and grabbed for a pen. He wrote, of course, the word "RESPECT" in purple ink and then looked intently at Tonya. "Can you build on this, Tonya? Who is respected? Who respects?"

"I respect the students, and they respect me—or at least that's what should happen."

"Okay. Any other dimensions to the respect?" The professor tapped the pen in the palm of his hand, waiting while Tonya struggled to get her focus.

"Well, like we talked about before, I have to respect myself and what I'm doing. And I owe respect to the school and the system and—"

Dr. Michaels couldn't wait for Tonya to come up with the exact words he wanted. "Yes, yes! I express it this way:" And he continued to talk as he wrote, in green ink, under RESPECT:

- For yourself
- For your students
- For the situation
- For the profession

"That's so important," Tonya broke in, "that part about the situation and the profession. The situation I see as the classroom and what we are expected to do there, me as the teacher, and them as the students working together. The profession is teaching and the system that supports it. If we as teachers don't honor our profession, how can we expect our students to respect us as professionals?"

"Exactly. By honoring and respecting our profession, we say to the world, or at least to the students and others we touch, that teaching—good teaching—is important and valuable and honorable."

"You do say that, Dr. Michaels, and I believe this is why people who have been your students have respect for you. It goes around."

"That's the point."

"I already have respect for the profession and for the situation and, of course, for my students and myself. But what happens when I meet my own students for the first time next fall? How do I communicate that respect? How do I get it from them?

"Obviously you did that this semester as a preservice teacher. What you did came naturally, from your sincerity. But you can extract the contributing factors if you look back. Think of our previous discussions. What attitudes and behaviors communicate respect?"

Dr. Michaels opened yet another pen, this time the black one—for serious emphasis. "Just one more thought from me, Ms. Simmons, before I listen to your ideas."

YOU CANNOT DEMAND RESPECT,

he wrote in large black letters.

YOU MUST COMMAND RESPECT.

"And how you command respect is what I am going to hear from you."

"Well, that brings us back to listening to the students, caring about them as individuals. I need to acknowledge their ideas and contributions—what they bring to the table. And I have to be accountable—to live up to the expectations I have for myself and for my students. That would mean following through on promises—being responsible to them."

"You are hitting the major ideas. Yes, integrity is essential if we are to gain respect."

"So," Tonya interjected, "what are some of the things—behaviors—you can extract from your experiences that might help me in earning my students' respect?"

"There was one idea I picked up from an accounting professor I had in college and adapted for my high school sophomores. Every day we would start with "social comment." They could bring up any thought they had had, a story from the news, something they had read or learned in another class—anything they wanted to talk about. No negatives were allowed. We all participated. We listened to each other. We acknowledged the value of what each other had to say.

That was one way. Then, of course, you must learn their names quickly and use them. And you must always pay attention. You are the mentor in your class. You will gain respect by knowing the emotional, physical, and psychological place of your students. Show that you care."

"But can't you get too involved with the students' personal lives? We're always told as preservice teachers not to get personally involved."

"Knowing where and who your students are doesn't mean you are crossing the line into their private lives. Respect for your responsibility as a teacher, for your situation, and for the profession means you know the difference between genuine caring and being a buddy. You are a teacher. Your responsibility is to teach and theirs is to learn, and you can do this with knowledgeable, professional caring. They expect, and respect, that a teacher honor her position and play her role. When you lose control, you will lose respect."

"Ah. That brings me to something else I wanted to discuss. I have known so many teachers—and there are some in my preservice program—who seem to want to be popular or something. It's like they have this enormous ego that needs to be bowed to. They, like, show off all the time and really go on a power trip. It's all about them, it seems, and not what the students are learning. They call all the shots—and the students better fall in line, or they get busted. More power tripping."

"Yes, Ms. Simmons. You have hit on one of the challenges to our profession—teachers who are there for themselves before they are available to their students."

"So, any ideas or suggestions? I never want to be one of those teachers."

"I read an observation once, in the book *Ordinary People,* or I heard it in the movie. Basically, the point was that when someone is being difficult for us, we must consider that what he or she is doing is an expression of himself or herself and not an act directed at—or against—us. I like that concept. We, as teachers, must depersonalize to be effective for our students. We need to leave our egos at the door and be totally open to what our students say and what they need to learn."

"I think that takes some real effort, especially the leaving your ego at the door part. I know I have an ego, and I want to know I'm in charge and that the kids are with me—and for me. I guess I need to keep reminding myself that I'm there for my students, not that my students are there for me." Tonya looked at her watch with surprise. "It's been an hour already, Dr. Michaels. I just get so revved."

"Don't worry about the time. I'm not. Neither one of us has classes next week, and I get pretty revved myself talking about teaching. It makes me realize how important it is to be a teacher, and a good teacher. So, what are you thinking now?"

"How do respect and discipline relate? I'm afraid of the discipline thing. Will students get out of hand if they don't respect you—and how can you make them behave?"

"Here's a story. Back when I was a high school teacher, the school had a field trip to a museum planned for all sophomores. My group went the same day as another teacher's, a guy who bellowed and strutted and thought he was prince of the world. We waited in the busses for everyone to arrive. I talked to the students about what we would see and how it would relate to what we were studying. The bus doors were open, and I heard that other teacher reading the riot act to his kids—what would happen if they did this or that, anticipating, of course, that they were preparing to trash the displays and then escape from the grounds or whatever. Well, I had no problem with my students. They were respectful to the guides and paid attention to the exhibits. His kids rampaged, and he bellowed. What does that tell you? Of course, I may have just been lucky, but I don't think so. Similar situations had the same results."

"You respected your students. You expected them to be responsible, and they honored that respect. He challenged his kids to challenge his authority. He didn't begin with respect. He disrespected them, and they responded. I see your point. Hope I can do it like you did." Tonya thought for a while and then added to her original concern. "Respect gives you power, is that right? Is power what you need to be a good teacher?"

"Respect gives your authority. And yes, a teacher has power. But that power can be abused. Having power can be a real ego trip for some teachers. Ultimately, I believe, the students feel exploited and respect breaks down."

"I'm not sure I quite get it, Dr. Michaels. Can you give me an example?"

"Yeah, sure. This one's about me.

"I learned a power lesson when I was a new social studies teacher at a middle school. The school was crowded, and we held classes in the multipurpose room with those pullout partitions separating the classrooms. I had my kids in the palm of my hand—they loved the class. However, the teacher on the other side of the partition—a Miss Halcomb—didn't have control of her group, and they made all kinds of noise, loud outbursts followed by Miss Halcomb yelling at the top of her voice for them to 'settle down.'

"One afternoon while we were having a serious discussion about the Spanish Civil War, the noise got to me. I told my students to go over and bang as hard as they could on the partition wall and then get back to their seats and not say a word. At my signal, they went over, pounded on the wall, then returned to their seats. A few minutes later, Miss Halcomb, red in the face and fuming, came into my classroom and demanded of the students to know what was going on. They sat silent as I had instructed. Then she turned to me and said, 'You'll hear about this!'"

"And did you?" Tonya asked.

"You bet. At the end of the day the department head stopped by my classroom to "have a word." He began by noting how well I was doing and how much the students liked my classes. Then he delivered his message. I had, all teachers have, power over their students. When we abuse that power, we abuse our students. I had abused my power. I had asked them to do something I shouldn't have had them do. It was my responsibility to deal with Miss Halcomb on my own, not to use them to do it for me. He made his point."

"I don't believe you would do that!" Tonya exclaimed. "What made you do something like that? Didn't you realize?"

"Not at the time, but I do now. I guess I just got carried away with the power I had to make my students do what I wanted. I wasn't respectful of them—and I could have lost their respect."

"What did you do? What happened?"

"I talked to them about it—during 'Social Comment' time. I admitted that what I had done was wrong—and I apologized. One of those situations when we learn right along with our students."

"Wow, I wonder what I'd do. Maybe find some way to laugh about it. Would that be appropriate?"

The professor had resumed his place at the desk, both elbows resting on an unorganized distribution of papers. He smiled. "Humor is a wonderful ally in the classroom. Being able to take your work seriously and yourself lightly is a real asset. You could laugh with your students at the wrongness of the situation without dismissing its significance."

"I'm always a bit afraid to be funny. I think they won't take me seriously—that I'll lose respect if I'm always telling jokes."

"Humor doesn't mean telling jokes. Good healthy humor means you can laugh—together—at foibles and situations, in a respectful way. Laughing with your students brings you together."

"I know I need to lighten up. I think when I have more confidence, I can let go a bit."

"You will, but don't wait until you're a year from retirement to give it a try."

"For sure."

"Actually, I do have an appointment. Now that school's out, what's your schedule?"

"I have two seminars this summer, but I still have Friday afternoons free."

"You've gotten me thinking about this whole teaching thing. I'd like to keep going—bring up some other ideas I've been turning around. We just might be building a new course here, Tonya!"

"Great. I really appreciate what I'm learning. Should I be doing something for next time?" Tonya collected the notes her students had written and put them back in her pocket.

Michaels stood up and waited for Tonya to walk to the door. "Just pay attention to what's going on," he offered by way of good-bye. "Like Yogi Berra said, 'You can observe a lot just by watching.'"

Conversation Points

1. How does a classroom teacher garner respect?

2. What can you do in your class to make an environment of respect the norm?

3. Leading by positive example is one way to gain external respect for the profession. How else will you promote respect for the profession?

CONVERSATION SIX

Observation

In the fields of observation, chance favors only the prepared mind.

—Louis Pasteur

It was the first Friday afternoon of summer break. Dr. Michaels was, apparently, emptying files and reorganizing his journals and books when Tonya made it to the third floor. His attitude seemed as casual as his attire—Bermuda shorts and a T-shirt proclaiming, "Buy Green!"

"Hello," Tonya offered, opening her pack and pulling a book Michaels had loaned her after their discussion of Pat Conroy's comment on teaching from *The Prince of Tides*. "Thanks for the books," she said. " I finally had a chance to read *The Water Is Wide*. A teacher can be so important, and Conroy writes so well, with real concern and passion."

"Yes. He's a wonderful observer of detail, don't you think?"

"All good writers must be good observers. How they react to what they observe and how they communicate it to us is what sets them apart."

"And good teachers, too. A good teacher is a good observer." The professor leaned back in his chair and crossed his arms over his chest. "So, Ms. Simmons, tell me about the kids in your classroom last semester."

"What do you want to know?"

"What did you observe? What details jumped out. What did you learn from watching?"

"They were a pretty average bunch, I guess. That girl who wrote the note was shy and got all embarrassed when she had to participate. A few kids were pierced all over, and I often wondered if it hadn't hurt to be punctured so many times—especially through the tongue. One girl wore a ribbon in her hair like Alice in Wonderland."

"So? What do you think about what you observed?"

"I learned the names of the kids who stood out faster than I did the ones who blended in."

"Yes, you noticed and you remembered them as individuals. All students want to be recognized and known. Some just have more obvious ways of expressing this need."

"Should I make comments, let them know what I notice?" Tonya seemed concerned about how she should react to what she observed.

"I believe you should. Let them know you see them, you realize when someone has a new haircut, you notice who they hang with. The way they dress can say a lot about what they like to do outside your classroom—the skate boarders, the musicians, the bikers. Take an interest. Acknowledge the individual."

Tonya still didn't seem sold on the idea. "Wouldn't I be intruding? Disrespecting their space?"

"Not if you aren't offering opinions—judgments. Noticing says you care and goes a long way in developing the rapport that supports good team learning." Michaels stood up and walked over to open the window. "What kinds of shoes are the kids wearing now? What about the kids who don't have backpacks. What are they saying? What music is associated with the different groups in your school?"

"I really can't answer. I was responsible for teaching certain topics, and that's where I put my attention. What seemed to matter most was whether they were with me, paying attention and getting involved. I didn't notice the other stuff so much."

"Well, I'm sure they appreciated your efforts and your honest concern for the subject. However, you may be able to form an even stronger connection when you use your skills of observation to validate the individuals in your classroom." Once he had the window adjusted just as he wanted, the professor resumed his seat and launched into a story.

"The last year I spent at the junior high school, I had a student, Liz, who dressed only in black. Today that might not be so unusual, but back then, it was. The other teachers ignored her, but I noticed and made lighthearted comments every day. I would say, 'Hey, Liz, I see you got on your spring black today.' I had to let her know

I noticed. Not to notice would have been to deny who she was. I got a lot of mileage out of that with her."

"Okay, I get it. It's like my friend, Hilary. She had this long, thick, brown hair, and she wore it so it fell all over her face when she leaned forward at her desk. One teacher noticed what she was doing with her hair. It was Mrs. Spaulding, and she wrote a note in the journals we had to turn in about how Hilary was hiding behind her hair. Mrs. Spaulding was the teacher who made Hilary care about school. They still keep in touch." Tonya twisted a tuft of her hair. "But we can't do that for every student."

"No, not that dramatically, but all we have to do is observe one or two details and connect these observations with individual students—people. It helps the students become real for us and reinforces caring and respect in our classrooms."

"It seems as if it would take so much effort, but I see the value."

"And the importance of observation isn't limited to your students in your classroom," Michaels commented, warming up to the discussion. "You can learn a lot by observing in the hall. Plenty of lessons are out there when you're paying attention."

"Makes me think of what you said about listening and paying attention. So often we don't really hear what someone else is saying because we are waiting for our turn to talk."

"Just like you told me before: 'Are you speaking to be heard, or listening for understanding?'"

"Exactly! When I first started paying attention to what I was hearing, I was astounded by what I could learn!" The professor reached into his lower drawer for a bottle of water and offered one to Tonya. As he twisted off the cap, he launched into another story.

"When I was a new teacher, I would walk the halls during class change and listen to what the kids were talking about—the TV shows, the music groups, soccer, other teachers. I saw who grouped together. I read the bulletin boards and noted what kids had taped up inside their lockers." He looked hopefully at Tonya, wanting assurance that she was with him.

"Yeah, I can see where that would be important. You get a sense of their environment that way, the culture they relate to."

"That's it. And I learned from observing the teachers, too. I noticed how the kids would rush into some classrooms and hang back from entering others. I saw teachers who stood near the door to their rooms and greeted the kids—often by noting something about the individuals, like a new jacket or a sports jersey or something. I decided I wanted to be a teacher whose classroom they rushed into, and I determined to learn what made them want to be in those environments."

"That makes so much sense. We can learn by observing what is out there and what works. It all goes back to paying attention. To caring about the whole person. About respecting and validating our students."

Michaels allowed himself a slow smile. "Yes, you are putting it together, Ms. Simmons." As he said this, he got out of his chair and positioned himself in front of his whiteboard. "So, in keeping with our habit, I will write on the board the word that sums up today's discussion. Give me that word, please."

"Observation," Tonya answered immediately.

"Can you be more direct, more active?" the professor goaded, comfortable in the challenging mode.

"Observe. That tells us what to do, how to act. Observe. Pay Attention. And I guess we can add, Learn." She watched as he wrote "OBSERVE," "PAY ATTENTION," and "LEARN" on the board in bright green letters.

And that was it for the afternoon. Dr. Michaels had a court time for tennis, and Tonya was leaving from their session to drive home for the weekend. Before saying good-bye, Tonya asked whether there was a subject to be thinking about for next week.

"Just observe, pay attention," the professor responded as he straightened a stack on his desk.

"But we're not in session. I don't have any students."

"True, but you aren't only a teacher of math and Spanish. You are a teacher of life. Observe, pay attention to where you are and who is around you. Then we can talk next week about what you learned. You'll be surprised."

Conversation Points

1. How will becoming a good observer play a significant role in your teaching process?

2. What have you observed to date that will affect your classroom?

3. How do you think your students perceive you? What are they observing?

Cultural Awareness

The first step in understanding how the culture of others affects one's thinking, values, beliefs, perceptions, and behaviors is to understand one's own culture.

—Gary Weaver

"Here you are, good afternoon!" Dr. Michaels stopped dropping papers into his file cabinet and looked at Tonya. She was as casually dressed as he, wearing for her part a short-sleeved T-shirt and red overall shorts with the straps hanging.

His shirt said, "I voted."

As always, her backpack was bulging. After sitting down and shifting its weight to her lap, she opened the top and pulled out a folder fat with pages torn from newspapers, magazines, and all other forms of printed material. "This is what I brought for today," she announced with a pleased smile. "Lots of pictures and words."

"Ah ha! A veritable show and tell!" Michaels responded, ready to start sifting through the folder. "I see you have been observing—am I on the right track?"

"I have, and it has been fascinating. I go to the mall and follow the teenagers to see what they're buying—or looking at. I listen to them at the food court. I check out who's hanging out with whom and what their connections seem to be. It's like doing research! I had no idea I could learn so much just by paying attention."

"Good for you," the professor encouraged. "And what have you learned? And why the folder?"

"Well," Tonya said opening the folder and handing Dr. Michaels a newspaper clipping, "I didn't want to be walking around with a camera, so I let the news photographers do it for me. This is a crowd shot of people waiting to get in to a concert. Good hair shots—and clothes, and check that attitude!"

"That attitude may well be in your first-period class next fall," Dr, Michaels offered with a knowing grin. "Be prepared."

"Yes, but I wouldn't want to confront her and be on the defensive. I'm aware, so I will be prepared to pay more attention and find out what she's all about. A bit like your student in black."

"You remembered," Michaels said with a slight twist of his head. "You have observed and now you will be prepared to observe some more and to listen. Observing, I guess you could say, is the first step in cultural awareness. We watch and we observe that something is different, not like us." He seemed to be holding back, not wanting to turn the session into a lecture, but he continued anyway. "Our first response when we encounter someone different, often with people from other cultures, is to make them like us so we will have an easier time dealing with them. I don't mean we set out to fix them, its more a mind thing. We assume they are like us, and we dismiss what is different." Michaels produced two bottles of juice and handed one to Tonya. "We miss so much—we deny so much when we do that. Individuals are different, we all accept that fact. Individuals grow up in different cultures with different values and behaviors and we need to appreciate the cultural context. We need to recognize and validate cultural heritage just as we recognize and validate the individual. How can we teach all our students if we can't reach them, or if we turn them off with our ignorance and insensitivity?"

"Or with our biases or prejudices," Tonya added, leaning forward over her pack as she did when she was really getting into a discussion. "That song from *South Pacific*—as old as it is, it tells it true, that children have to be taught to hate. While they're very young, they are taught by their relatives to hate people who are different from them, whether it's their skin, their eyes, their family culture, or whatever it is that's different."

Michaels began talking before Tonya had finished. "Are we talking about racism here or cultural awareness?" He paused to reflect. "Perhaps by observing and learning, we can increase our awareness and we can unlearn, or relearn the assumptions that have kept us separate from our students."

"As a teacher," Tonya offered with an assurance that suggested she had put some thought into this issue before, "paying attention and learning about differences is our obligation, if I can use that word. It is our responsibility to our students to care about difference, to learn, and to clean our filters so we can see clearly." She seemed pleased with her position and continued, "We do this to become better teachers, and examples for our students. Didn't you say that we are mentors for our students? We can mentor by showing them that we want to be more culturally aware." She sighed and slid down in her chair.

"Keep going, Tonya," Michaels encouraged. "It's good to hear what one of our new teachers will be bringing to her classroom."

"Okay, well," Tonya twisted the strap of her overalls, "it's also important to learn what we don't know so we can be receptive to new understanding." She let herself drift a bit, then came back. "People assume that because I am African American, I know all about African American culture. 'You can talk to him, or to her,' they would say at the middle school, 'You come from the same background'—or something to that effect. Not true!" Tonya was becoming adamant. "I grew up in the Midwest. I don't know about Oakland, California, or Birmingham, Alabama."

Dr. Michaels steepled his fingers, giving Tonya a nod to continue.

"I learned that lesson fast when I was a counselor that summer at a church retreat camp. That's when I realized that to be effective as a counselor, let alone a teacher, I had to observe and listen and learn. I couldn't rely on my learned biases or assumptions if I was to be real for those kids." A smile introduced her next thought. "How could I be genuinely caring if I couldn't be open enough to learn? What is it you say? 'Are you listening for understanding, or speaking to be heard?'"

Dr. Michaels caught the reference to himself and acknowledged it with a quick grin. "You, Ms. Simmons," he said with an avuncular tone, "have been preparing for a long time to be a good teacher."

"Well, in that sense, I guess I have. I also listen to stories about what other people have experienced and—I hope—learn from them." She sat back up in her seat and assumed a storytelling demeanor. "This was my cousin's experience, not mine, but it told me something about where we all started out—before we had any racial or cultural awareness."

The professor leaned forward on his elbows and encouraged her to tell the story.

"He—Dean—was in Guatemala doing an intense language program. He had this friend, Jen, who was, as they called her, a perfect 'golden girl,' the long, blond hair, the big blue eyes, all that. Dean is African American to start with, but after a few weeks in that sun, he was definitely darker. The two of them planned a trip to a remote village to check out what they had heard about a natural dyeing process. While they were there, two little kids followed them around. Jen asked if she could take their picture. After the photo, the little boy shyly asked her a question. My cousin didn't hear the question, but he did see Jen start to laugh. 'What did he want?' Dean asked her. 'They wanted to know if we were brother and sister!' Jen responded, as dumbfounded as Dean."

"And?" queried the professor.

"Well, to me it said that the kids had no preconceived notions about color or race. I realize we all start out that way. Then we learn. To some degree, how our students keep on learning is up to us." Tonya slumped back again, feigning exhaustion to mask what was really exhilaration.

"Wow, I'm talking a lot this afternoon," she added as a coda. "We've leapt from observing at the mall to a defense of cultural awareness, to the tabula rasa of our innocence."

"It all fits," the professor added with confidence. "We're talking about becoming aware. Being culturally aware is a necessary condition for good teaching."

"Did I tell you," Tonya asked, slipping her heels out of the heavy sandals she wore, "that I spent a year in Japan after graduating from college as part of the JET program? It's a program set up by the Japanese government to bring young people from other countries to teach their languages and cultures to Japanese students. I was in a prefecture not far from Kobe. I was supervised by a regular teacher, but I presented my own lessons for English students."

"Wonderful, Tonya. I had not realized you'd had that experience—an excellent preparation for continuing cultural awareness. I wish every teacher could travel and experience other cultures directly."

Tonya visibly warmed to the subject. "Talk about observing!" she all but exploded, "I observed for survival. I had to figure out what was going on if I was to create effective lessons, one-time lessons. And they observed me, the only African American in the prefecture. That was one thing about Japan. I, well all the JETS, got stared at wherever we went. The farther we were from the Hollywood stereotype the more stares we got—in the store, on the train, on the street. But that was the point. Let the Japanese students learn about another culture by observing—up close and personal!"

"And, Ms. Simmons, or should I say Tonya *sensei*, what did you observe of your new culture?" Dr. Michaels fixed his gaze on the back of his hands. He was in a listening mode.

"Let me limit it to what I observed that affected my teaching, or my lessons. First I learned that the students were reluctant to participate for fear of looking like they wanted to stand out—be noticed. There is a Japanese saying about how the nail that sticks up will be hammered down. That awareness made me sensitive to not putting a student on the spot and embarrassing him. I often had kids do things in groups." Tonya grabbed the water bottle and took a few gulps. "I learned from watching my lead teacher that she mostly talked to them; they didn't participate much. I asked about this and I learned that many Japanese students have learned it is disrespectful to question their elders. It's pretty ingrained. They are very respectful of authority, more so than I had been as a teenager, for sure!"

"And you will carry that awareness into your classes. And just as you have learned about Japanese culture by observing in Japan, you can continue to learn about the cultural background of students in your classes at Sequoia High. You know, there is a concentration of Hmong families in Katonville, an Asian culture quite different from Chinese or Korean, or even Vietnamese."

"I have already started to learn what I can. That's where the newspapers come in. The local paper carries articles about city housing issues and language challenges and celebrations that will give me insight. At least they will help me be a better observer. And they will give me a chance to let the students know that I am paying attention, that I want to learn who they are, that I am interested, and that I respect their differences." Tonya was getting wound up, her back getting straighter and her hand gestures going into double time.

"But those kids represent the obvious cultural differences. There are plenty more cultures going on in a classroom," Michaels interjected as a goad.

"Tell me about it!" She pressed her hands on the arms of her chair as if she was getting ready to stand up, then decided against it and relaxed back in the chair, her pack still on her lap. "I went to a high school with lots of cliques, different economic groups, and a spattering of races and ethnicities. I shifted from one culture group to the other because I always wanted to have 'United Nations'–type friendships. There was the 'good student' group, the basketball women, the Students of Color organization, and the Ridge Hill kids. The Ridge Hill kids had mostly professional parents, and we were all supposed to have the same attitudes and values. Some teachers couldn't get beyond the assumption that we were all snobs."

"And what did you learn from that experience that you can use as a teacher?" the professor asked, clearly interested in what Tonya's answer would be. He had stopped shuffling the papers on his desk and was looking directly at his student.

"That as a teacher you need to pay attention to the culture of the moment as well as the background culture," Tonya answered with assurance. "You can use those identities positively by showing interest and learning how those roles—or cultures—play out in your classroom mix." She wriggled her feet back into the sandals." I really noticed those teachers who could shift with me—who recognized all the people I was—and didn't limit me with their first assumptions."

"Respecting each group and culture is at the heart of teaching, don't you think?" The professor served the ball into Tonya's court.

"Yes, but what about the drugs and the gangs and that stuff?" Tonya spoke slowly. She seemed concerned. "Those groups have a culture, too. Should we learn about them and respect that culture as well?" Tonya had become quiet and serious, looking to Professor Michaels for an answer.

"A good question, Tonya," Michaels began, accepting his turn in the discussion. "Gang culture, drug culture, even some aspects of the jock culture are not what we want to condone, but we will never have a chance to learn with our students if we don't learn first ourselves. Again, don't assume. Observe, listen, ask, and pay attention. What values do the cultures have? Can we work with those values?" Michaels paused, uncertain how to go on and clearly aware that he had not given a satisfactory response.

Tonya was aware of his hesitation and turned back to him with a new energy. "We need to be willing to stretch," she offered, "to become more than who we are in order to become more effective as teachers for all our students."

"And how will you accomplish this?" the professor queried in his Socratic voice. He took Tonya's moment of gathering her thoughts to move to the window and check the weather.

"I had this professor," Tonya began to respond, positioning herself to rise from the chair, "who had this Teacher Effectiveness Awareness Stretch model that made a lasting impression on me. I've got my notes here. I thought they might relate to what we were going to talk about today." She was out of her seat and on her way to the board when she caught herself. "May I?" she asked, picking up a purple pen.

"Go right ahead," Michaels smiled, "I'm with you."

Tonya drew what looked like a bar graph, starting from the left with the shortest column and moving to the highest. She labeled her columns, from left to right, UNAWARE, AWARE, ACCEPTANCE, UNDERSTANDING, and APPRECIATION.

"Okay," she paused and began to write as she talked. "This first one, UNAWARE, that refers to effective teaching practices, or, in today's context, to the value of cultural awareness in effective teaching. If you're here, you are simply unaware of what makes an effective teacher—either because you don't care or because no one has called your attention to what you need to know."

Next she moved to AWARE and drew two bullets. "To be aware of differences," she instructed as Michaels listened attentively, "you must train yourself to notice differences. That's what we've been talking about in cultural awareness. Then you should try to do something in response to the differences you notice. This isn't a passive game of observation."

Tonya made a gesture as if to shoot her sleeve, or straighten a stiff arm. "ACCEPTANCE," she pronounced. And drew three bullets. "At this stage in the Awareness Stretch," she continued, sounding for all the world like a seasoned teacher, "you need to reflect on those differences [first bullet], respect others' right to be different [second bullet], and accept that something needs to change if we are to be effective in the face of differences [third bullet]."

"And that something," the professor interjected, leaning back against the wall, "could be your attitude toward the difference, or simply accepting that the difference exists and may not be a bad thing. Remember that thought about someone's actions being an expression of themselves and not an act against you."

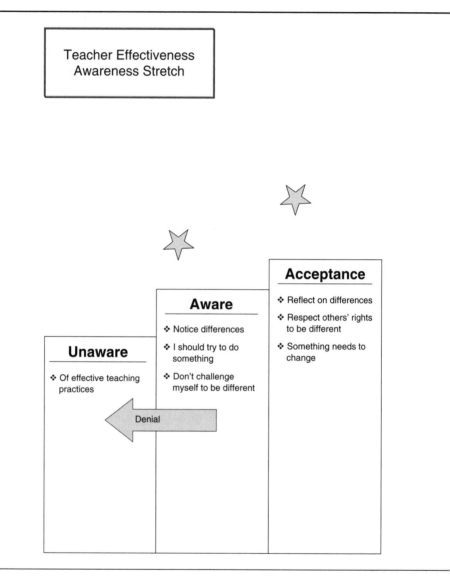

Figure 7.1   Teacher Effectiveness Awareness Stretch

Once you get to Appreciation, there should be a continuous exchange between appreciation and understanding.

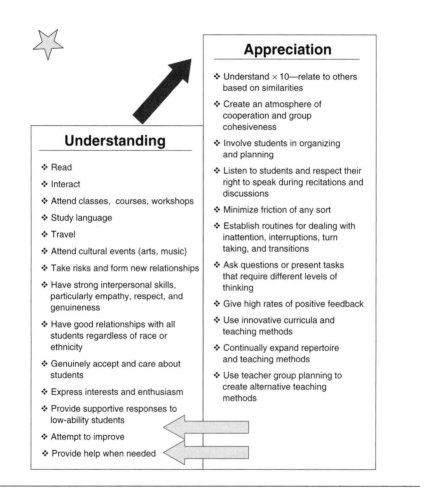

Appreciation

❖ Understand × 10—relate to others based on similarities

❖ Create an atmosphere of cooperation and group cohesiveness

❖ Involve students in organizing and planning

❖ Listen to students and respect their right to speak during recitations and discussions

❖ Minimize friction of any sort

❖ Establish routines for dealing with inattention, interruptions, turn taking, and transitions

❖ Ask questions or present tasks that require different levels of thinking

❖ Give high rates of positive feedback

❖ Use innovative curricula and teaching methods

❖ Continually expand repertoire and teaching methods

❖ Use teacher group planning to create alternative teaching methods

Understanding

❖ Read

❖ Interact

❖ Attend classes, courses, workshops

❖ Study language

❖ Travel

❖ Attend cultural events (arts, music)

❖ Take risks and form new relationships

❖ Have strong interpersonal skills, particularly empathy, respect, and genuineness

❖ Have good relationships with all students regardless of race or ethnicity

❖ Genuinely accept and care about students

❖ Express interests and enthusiasm

❖ Provide supportive responses to low-ability students

❖ Attempt to improve

❖ Provide help when needed

Conversation Points

1. Where are you on the "Awareness Stretch"?

2. Where would you like to be?

3. What are you willing to do to get there?

"Yes," Tonya said as way of acknowledging the professor's participation. "So the first challenge under UNDERSTANDING is 'Read.' To understand you can begin by reading—like the articles in the local paper about the Hmong. Next is to interact, be there, listen, observe. Next could be to take courses or workshops about, say, a culture you don't known much about. Then, of course, you could study the language, travel, attend cultural events." She was getting excited and talking at a rapid-fire rate. "To further the Understanding sphere, you can take risks and form new relationships. For a teacher, this doesn't mean forming personal relationships but developing good connections with students of all races, ethnicities, and interests. Genuine caring and acceptance goes without saying—at least in Professor Michaels' office," she said looking at him and smiling.

"Expressing interest and enthusiasm helps in making the valuable people-to-people connections. And finally, to express understanding, a teacher should provide supportive responses to every student and be open to provide help when it's needed."

Tonya took a breath and looked at the professor and then the board. "I don't know how I'll fit all this in, but I'll do the best I can." She began with the green pen.

"APPRECIATION, the last step in the Awareness Stretch." Tonya appeared to stretch herself to reach the top of the APPRECIATION column. "First, relate to others based on how you are similar. We are alike in wanting to learn, in caring about the subject, in caring about the world."

Dr. Michaels took a step forward as if with body language he could interrupt Tonya's progression. "Cultural differences," he began, "human similarities." The professor, aware that he had successfully halted Tonya for the moment, went on with what he wanted to say.

"Here's a story for you." He stood tall, rotating what might have been a sore shoulder. "I was with a group of teachers in Soweto, South Africa, a few years back, over the summer. As I said earlier, travel is a great opportunity for learning. We had arrived early in the morning at a small village where the people had almost nothing, bits of clothing, chickens scratching in the dry dirt. The school was a one-room shack. Then the teacher rang the bell and from every crack and corner and shanty came barefoot, grinning little brown boys and girls running to school!" The professor smiled to himself at the memory. "Does that remind you of anything, Tonya?"

"Yes," she responded, "it reminds me of what you observed at the high school. The kids running to certain teachers and their classrooms. That excitement about learning. They are either going to run to you or away from you. What you're saying is that loving to learn is the human similarity. And also," she added with a note of thoughtfulness, "that it is our trust as teachers to keep that energy and love of learning alive."

"That was how it struck me," the professor concluded. "As different as our worlds and experiences were, we found in South Africa the same desire to learn that we have here in the U.S." He looked as if he were going to say more, but instead he indicated that Tonya should continue with her model.

"Thanks for the story," Tonya acknowledged with sincerity. "So, okay," she looked at her notes. "Next," she said, getting back in gear, "as teachers we need to create an atmosphere of cooperation and group cohesiveness. Then we must involve all students from all backgrounds in organizing and planning. We also must listen and respect each student's right to speak and be heard. It is up to us to minimize friction among students. The more we understand, the better we can recognize and respond." At this point Tonya switched to curious shorthand and promised the professor a copy of the original model.

"Next, establish a routine for dealing with distractions and interruptions that includes and respects everyone. Give positive, honest feedback to encourage everyone to participate. And finally, based on our acquired understanding, we must appreciate what we have learned about individual and cultural differences and continue to seek innovative curricula and teaching methods to meet the needs of all our students."

"Phew," she added as final punctuation. "I'm afraid I sounded like a lecturer. I didn't let you get involved much."

"Oh," the professor said, "but I was listening and thinking and, I guess you could say, waiting my turn."

"Any comment?" Tonya asked, still standing in front of the board and holding the green pen.

"We've had a long ride today," the professor began, "from observing kids at the mall to being stared at in Japan to becoming aware of cultures in our classrooms and identities in our students." He chuckled to himself in a muffled sort of way. "Observing takes work and energy. Cultural awareness takes sensitivity and openness to difference. To be effective teachers we must continue to learn—and not be judgmental in the process. We learn with our students about each other and about ourselves. That's how we become good teachers—and better teachers than we were yesterday or last week."

"And so," Tonya held back as to not appear to be interrupting, "speaking of next week—"

"Actually my words were 'last week,' but go on," said the professor, still smiling.

"I won't be here. I'll be at the shore observing seagulls and waves. But I'm up for any assignment and hope we can meet in two weeks. Fall is approaching fast."

"Good opportunity to talk about balance. Teaching can be draining, exhausting work. We need to be careful to take care of ourselves, to replenish and reenergize ourselves or we court burnout. Enjoy your vacation, and I'll see you in two weeks."

"Thank you. I hope you'll take a break yourself! I'll see you in two."

Tonya left the office and Dr. Michaels went back to filing his papers. The folder of pictures and news clippings Tonya had forgotten caught his attention, and he began to go through the stack, pausing to read a passage or study a photograph.

Conversation Points

1. How do you increase your level of cultural awareness?

2. How will you get your students to appreciate the cultural differences that are present in the classroom?

3. If you had the opportunity to have an Awareness Stretch, what would you do?

CONVERSATION EIGHT

Balance

Anyone can steer the ship when the sea is calm.

—Publius Syrus

Tonya was sitting on the floor, her back against the wall and her backpack on her knees, when Dr. Michaels appeared at the end of the corridor all but trotting in the direction of his office.

"Sorry, sorry! Our match went late. I won." The professor unzipped his tennis case looking for his keys. "So, how was wave watching?"

"What a great vacation," Tonya answered, getting to her feet and shifting the pack to her shoulder. "I just kind of mused and stared out at the water and swam a bit and ran a lot and slept and ate excellent food—and got engaged."

"And we were going to talk about balance! A month from now you start your first teaching job, and to that you're adding getting married! You, Ms. Simmons, are facing some real challenges." Michaels set his tennis racket on the floor and reached into his bottom drawer for two bottles of water before collapsing into his chair with mock exhaustion. He handed Tonya one.

"I did remember to bring you something. Remember, I bring something to the table?" Tonya pulled a square package from her backpack and handed it to the professor.

"For me?" Michaels smiled at his trite response while proceeding to unwrap the gift.

"This is wonderful, Tonya, but perhaps you should keep it—it's for you too." He held the wood framed photograph at arm's length then brought it in for a closer examination. "Yes, this is it. This is what we want to keep alive or to kindle again."

"When I saw it in the shop, I knew it was for you. You gave me the image in my head," Tonya said, "and with the photo I can give it back to you in an image you can see every day." And she added as an afterthought, "Not that you need to be reminded."

"Kids running. I'd say they are nine or ten. We don't see what they are running toward, but the eagerness and joy on their faces is what we want to see when they are running toward us—toward their teachers." He rested the framed photograph against some books stacked on his shelf. "The photographer recognized that spirit and caught it. Thank you, Tonya."

"You're welcome, Dr. Michaels."

Both professor and student were quiet for a while, glancing at the photograph and avoiding each other. Then Tonya broke the silence.

"The last two weeks felt so good, kind of restorative, but toward the end I was getting anxious to be back. Back here, back preparing for my classes and my students." Tonya waited politely for Dr. Michaels to take up the theme, and he did.

"I'm glad you took the break, Tonya, and I hope you will continue to take care of yourself and live a whole life even as you feel more and more deeply drawn into the demands of your students." The professor fanned his fingers and brought them together in a steeple. "It's easy to become immersed in the details and emotions of teaching. Like we've said, you have a commitment and a mission, and you care—about students as people and about how they are learning. I can remember when I was a young teacher: I would become almost obsessed with, say, how I was communicating about the Civil War. I worried about a particular student and why he seemed so unengaged. I reworked lesson plans in my head while my wife—my wife at the time—and I were out for dinner with friends. I got out of bed and all but ran to my desk with a thought or a new way to approach the Battle of Gettysburg. I did not conceive of time that was not devoted to—to being a teacher."

"That's total dedication, Dr. Michaels. That must have had something to do with your reputation for being such a good teacher."

"No, Ms. Simmons, it was too much. I still had only 50 minutes a day with each class. It was who I was in the classroom that mattered. Yes, I had to be prepared, and, yes, for first-year teachers that preparation can take hours outside the classroom. But I also had to be a full person, a person alive in the world and observing. Not only observing my students, but the world we were living in so I could legitimately make what we were doing in the classroom relevant to the world."

"And if all you can see is the classroom and the students, you are remote from the outside world." Tonya seemed to take energy from responding to her professor. "When you were trying to save the world by becoming involved in politics and policy outside of school, you were denying your students your attention. When you were in your earliest days obsessed with your classroom, you were denying your students the world." Tonya seemed pleased with her speech—especially with the parallelism she had created.

"And don't forget one's personal life, and health, and growth. As we mature as whole people, we bring that example and that learning into our classrooms as well." The professor had recovered his ground and again felt in charge—at least of his half of the conversation. He allowed himself a light tilt back in the chair and waited for Tonya to take her turn.

"This, then, is the balance you wanted to talk about." Tonya sounded a bit patronizing, and she knew it, but she sat back and waited for the professor to lead.

"Yes," Michaels drew out the word as he reached for his tennis case and unzipped the ball pocket. "And, I neglected a moment ago to say congratulations, ask when the event will happen, and inquire as to what I will be calling you. Still Simmons? Or will you be Mrs. Evans, or something hyphenated?"

"I—or should I say we—haven't decided on my name. But I'll still be Tonya, so go with that." Tonya smiled and warmed to the new subject. "He's staying for his PhD and working hard on his dissertation, so I doubt if he'll notice what I call myself."

"And, then, Ms. Simmons—for now—back to balance." At this point, the professor took three tennis balls from the case and looked directly at Tonya.

"There is a difference," he began with his authoritative tone, "between juggling and balance." Tonya nodded to indicate she was with him. "We hear so much about 'juggling priorities' and 'juggling responsibilities.' What does juggling really mean?

"Let's name the tennis balls, Ms. Simmons. What are some of the responsibilities you'll have next year?"

Tonya was getting into the demonstration, leaning toward the desk, her face showing interest. "Obviously teaching is a big one," she offered. "And my upcoming marriage, and I want to keep running at least 20 miles a week. And then," she paused to ask the professor whether she could go beyond the three balls and received his okay. "And then, I want to learn how to cook, and I found a drumming group I want to join, and I love to read, and I have my nieces and nephews and love to spend time with them, and—"

The professor interrupted by standing up and silencing Tonya with a hand gesture. "So," he stood tall, "we'll take the teaching ball and the marriage ball and the drumming ball."

He threw first one, then the other two balls in the air and to his—and Tonya's—amazement, began to juggle. "Watch what is happening," he instructed.

"You're doing it!" Tonya exclaimed.

"Yes," rejoined the professor, "but how? Note that all three balls are in the air at one time. I am not touching any of them." That noted, he lost control and the balls bounced off the desk and rolled around the floor. "And then I lose control. That," he said, "is juggling. You lose touch, and you lose control."

"And balance?" asked Tonya, totally into the show.

"Balance," Michaels pronounced, "is a different approach." He further unzipped the tennis case and brought out the racket, which he balanced on his upturned index finger." This is balance. I know how to apportion the weight. I am in touch with the racket the whole time. I am in control."

"Then I'd better learn to balance and not how to juggle." Tonya smiled and settled back in her chair. "Pretty simple concept, but I know I'll be thinking about it this week. I'll get the feel for when I'm trying to juggle and when I am working on balance. Is it okay if I say that balance seems more grounded?" She offered the professor a pleased-with-herself smile.

"Touché, Tonya." The professor smiled back. "And what shall we discuss next week—if next week is still on your schedule?"

"The people who had you in high school and the ones I have met here at the university tell me how they remember being in your class, liking to come to class, feeling good about what they were learning. They seem to always talk about 'we' studied this or 'we' did that. I want to know what you did in your classroom that made your students feel good about learning and about themselves." Tonya took a visible breath and went on with her request. "So far we've talked about attitudes and the more abstract elements that make a good teacher. Now I really want to hear from you about what you did, how you put your philosophy into play." Her expression became serious and receptive. "Would you do that, Professor?"

Dr. Michaels had resumed his seat, with his elbows on the desk. He picked up a pencil and balanced it on the back of his hand. "Sometimes it's more difficult for the person doing something to know what it is he's doing than it is for an observer to extract what he's doing. But I can tell you what I tried to do, what I tried to accomplish within my classroom. And I think you will see how my approach inside the classroom was—is—consistent with what you refer to as my philosophy."

"Thank you. And might it be all right if I bring a tape recorder? I'd always rather listen than take notes. And I don't want to miss anything." Tonya had begun gathering her things. Michaels stood and moved toward the door.

"That's fine. Maybe, if you get me a copy, I can listen to what I had to say—and learn something!" His eyes jumped to the framed photograph leaning against the books. "And, Ms. Simmons, thank you for the photo. I'll keep it where I can see it."

"Next week, then," Tonya said over her shoulder as she half closed the door behind her.

Conversation Points

1. Respond to the question, "Are you working to live or living to work?"

2. What will you do to ensure that your students are "balanced" in their approach to learning?

3. What is the difference for you between "juggling" and "balancing"?

CONVERSATION NINE

Teambuilding

The nice thing about teamwork is that you always have others on your side.

—Margaret Carty

D r. Michaels was in his office when Tonya came down the hall. The professor was intently moving stacks of papers and journals from the table abutting his desk and piling them in three boxes on the floor. He looked up when he heard Tonya approaching and greeted her with a standard "Hello, how's it going." Gesturing to the cleared table, he announced he was ready for her to set up the tape recorder.

"I've got it right here," Tonya told the professor while extracting a small microcassette dictator from her bag. This was the first time Michaels had seen Tonya without her bulky blue backpack. Instead, she had a brightly woven purselike carryall that she swung around to dig through while it remained attached to her by a wide shoulder strap.

Michaels noted the image adjustment. Cultural expression? Identity statement? Leaving the student behind to become the teacher?

"Great colors. I like that design," the professor offered as casually as he could muster.

"Thanks," Tonya responded. "A friend brought it back from Lesotho. I like it, too."

"So," Michaels thought to himself, "she likes it—the colors and the design. It's from Africa. Says something about her tastes and her choices. This young woman is ready to position herself. She's getting to know who she is. If she can keep a grip on that insight, she won't get lost in the student–teacher interactions."

"Can we get started, then?" Tonya asked, not making any effort to disguise her enthusiasm.

"You begin, Ms. Simmons. You're the investigator here. Like I tell my students, you are the detectives—the reporters. It's your job to think about what you want to learn and to look for answers and solutions. Then you can report back."

"Report back to whom?" Tonya asked, getting into the groove.

"To your team, to the class, to the teacher. You investigate and share the results of your investigation with the others." Michaels twirled in his chair as a way of ending his response before it turned into a chapter.

"Actually, Professor, you just got us going." Her smile revealed that she was pleased with herself for observing what had just happened. "We were going to talk about how you do it, how you teach. And you just told me that you encourage your students to be investigators—or, as you said, detectives. Then you said they would report back to a team, which you suggested meant the class and the teacher." She paused and when Michaels didn't say anything, she added, "Am I getting it?"

The professor waited a few seconds to let the realization "steep," as he liked to imagine the process. "I think we both are," he answered and waited for Tonya to take charge.

"I want to hear you talk more about teams, about teambuilding." Tonya stopped, waiting for the professor to leap in, and when he didn't respond immediately, she added, "That's what I hear from your former students. That you made them feel part of a team. We hear the terms 'teambuilding' and 'creating a team' all the time in our classes. But I want to know *why* and *how*."

"The investigator at work!" Dr. Michaels looked at Tonya with a thoughtful expression that eventually gave way to a smile. "Teams," he said, "that's how I see my classrooms full of students. We are teams, and I mean 'we' because I am a part of the team, too. We care about each other and what we are learning together. We respect everyone's responsibility to contribute and be heard."

"Okay, Professor, but why create a team feeling when you can also be caring and observing and listening and aware in a traditional teacher's role?" Tonya was talking fast, as if she was not totally comfortable pushing the professor for the answers she wanted to discover.

On his part, Dr. Michaels seemed to warm to the challenge. "Because," he ventured, "my experience has shown me that students learn best when they are engaged, when they are involved in the learning process rather than just passively receiving information."

"But why are they more engaged when they become a team?" Tonya was relaxing into her role as investigator and wasn't about to quit before she got her answer.

"Because they develop a sense of responsibility to each other when they are a team, as well as to their teacher who is, in a sense, a team leader. Like an athletic team, they want to win—or in the classroom, they want to succeed. Everyone contributes to the effort. If someone falls behind, it's a drag on the team, and the members rally to support and help out." Michaels stood up from his chair and began a slow pace from desk to window. "On a team, you belong. People know who you are. They care about you and you care about them. And together your goal is learning. You've got an identity with your team and you work to maintain that good identity." He nodded toward Tonya to indicate it was her turn.

"Okay," she began as a way of buying think time, "you are talking about building a community of students learning, and the community is made up of people with an interest in each other's success. They have team—or community—pride."

"Right," Michaels interrupted. "Sometimes I express it this way." He took one giant step and landed in front of the whiteboard. Taking up the black pen, he wrote "WII-FM" and stood back to admire his capital letters. "You know that expression?" he asked Tonya.

"For sure. My grandmother always responded, 'WII-FM?' whenever we asked her to do something or go someplace. It stands for What's In It For Me?"

"And your grandmother wanted to know there was a good reason for her act, or she wasn't about to go along or get involved." Now Michaels had the green pen, with which he wrote WII-FW. "I will not try to pronounce this one, but you get the idea. Individual students sitting together in a classroom ask WII-FM. The classroom team asks WII-FW—What's In It For We?

"When your whole classroom wants to know what's in it for them, you as a teacher have a great challenge to deliver. And when we as teachers include ourselves in the 'we,' we are vested in the outcome right along with our students." The professor couldn't resist an aggressive underlining of the WII-FM and WII-FW before he snapped the cap onto the pen and strolled over to rest his hands on the back of his chair.

"That will stay with me," Tonya said as she shifted her position and prepared to push the discussion along. "So," she smiled, "now that you have defended the learning justification for your classroom teams, how do you do it? How do you take a bunch of random kids and make them a team?" She waited.

"Let me tell you about a team I was part of." Michaels stood straight behind the chair, as if at respectful attention. "It was eighth grade. In our school, we were grouped by ability—or at least by performance—into seventeen sections, one being the highest. I was in section six. There were about fifteen of us, all boys. Like all kids that age, when we got into our assigned classroom, we checked each other out, slouched in our seats, and crossed our arms across our chests in a classic 'I dare you' pose. Our teacher introduced himself and then said something like, 'Well, Section Six, what do you think?'" Michaels nodded his head as if agreeing with himself. "He challenged us to tell him who we were. If we didn't know who we were, he said, nobody else was going to know us either! One kid— it wasn't me—ventured that we were Super Section Six. Someone added "Sonic' and we had Super Sonic Section Six. Within a few weeks, we were 'Super, Sonic, Superior, Spectacular, Soulful, Slick, Sophisticated, Sexy Section Six.'" Michaels delivered the sequence of S words in rapid fire.

"And that's how you became a team?" Tonya asked.

"That's one way. We shared an identity, and we were proud to be part of Section Six. When a couple of us had a chance to move up, we wanted to stay. Even now when we get together for reunions, we all remember supersonicsuperiorspectacularsoulfullslicksophis- ticatedsexysectionsix."

"What about learning?" Tonya wasn't about to give up before she had what she wanted. "Do you think being a team encouraged learning?"

"I never worked harder or paid better attention," Michaels answered with a pleased look, "I didn't want to let my team down. And because we felt like a team, I never hesitated to ask one of the other kids for help on a project. And no one held back from helping someone else. We weren't separate and competitive. We were in it together."

"Sounds good to me," Tonya responded. "In high school, we had a college composition class where I felt we were a team, a community. At the holidays, our teacher suggested that we each give something from ourselves to the class. I remember a girl named Rita made a drawing of hands and gave a copy to each of us. Eric brought his a capella group in to sing. Tally made those German Christmas cookies from her grandmother's recipe. Doug brought his dog that he'd trained to jump through hoops. Our teacher read a poem she had written. CJ and I tap danced. We really got to know each other that way. It made us a tight group—a team. And, honestly, I remember that when our term papers were due, we did naturally help each other. I even have a picture of our mass writing marathons!"

"And I have often," Michaels added, "simply had kids learn something about each other—a middle name, a favorite vegetable. Knowing is the first step in caring."

"For the teacher, too," Tonya interjected. "It's all fitting together. First you wanted me to think about my mission, why I wanted to be a teacher and what I wanted to accomplish. That started my focus. Then we talked about expectations—those I had for myself and those my students had for me. One of their expectations was for their teacher to be prepared. Being prepared applied to knowing the subject but also to being prepared to meet and mentor students and to facilitate their learning. Preparing for team learning would be part of that. And then power and a teacher's responsibility to respect her, or his, power. When you have a team, you share some of the power in the classroom. The teacher has to listen to understand who his or her students are and to hear what they're asking and what they need to learn. They can become investigators together and share the power of learning. Caring has to be at the center, genuine caring for who our students are and what they can become. And with caring comes respect we have for ourselves, for our students, and for the honor of being a teacher. To demonstrate our caring and respect, we must be culturally aware, we must be observers and preservers of what makes students run to us instead of away from us. The classroom teams are inclusive, with caring and respect for individuals and contributing cultures." Tonya sank back in her chair as if deflated, but quickly sat straight and looked at her professor, who was resting against the window ledge, his face indicating complete attention to what this new teacher was saying.

"Wow," he exclaimed softly. "Did we cover all that? Did you get all that from our discussions?"

"And more, all the stories and my memories of being a student, and my student teaching experiences that you helped me learn from." Not given to shyness, Tonya nevertheless seemed to be staring at her knees. "I don't think it stops here. I think you have given me ways to think about what I'm doing and the teacher I want to become."

"And you, Ms. Simmons, have challenged me to rediscover what teaching means—for me and for fine new teachers like you. Thanks to your listening and questioning and sharing your experiences and expectations, somehow I have become revitalized." Reflexively, as if to grab a life preserver in the rough seas of an awkward moment, the professor picked up a marker pen and twisted off the top. With the purple pen he wrote, in large capital letters, TEACHER and underlined it twice.

Tonya had put away the little recorder and stood beside her chair. "I start teaching in two weeks. Meetings start next week. But there is still so much to learn, and I know once I'm into it, I'll have more questions—and stories. Can I call you, and can we meet for coffee? And talk?"

"That would be good. Keep me tuned in, will you, Tonya? We can both continue to bring things to the table." The professor looked up as he heard a knock on his office door. He turned to Tonya, who was on her way out. "I thought no one else was here on a perfect August tennis afternoon!" Then he said, "Come in."

"Hello, excuse me for interrupting. I just took a chance . . ." The young man in shorts and woven sandals shifted his backpack from his shoulder to the floor. Dr. Michaels and Tonya looked at each other and smiled. Tonya slipped out the door, and the young man continued, "I'm starting as a preservice teacher in two weeks, and I've heard so much about you as a teacher, Dr. Michaels. I know how busy you are, but if you had some time, could we get together so I could ask you some questions?"

The professor gestured for the young student to take a seat and reached for the green pen.

Conversation Points

1. What does team mean to you?

2. What will you do to create a team atmosphere in your classroom?

3. What will be your . . . supersonicsuperiorspactacular-soulfulslicksophisticatedsexysectionsix?

CONVERSATION TEN

Growth and Knowledge

Challenges make you discover things about yourself that you never really knew. They're what make the instrument stretch—what make you go beyond the norm.

—Cicely Tyson

Tonya shuffled toward the picnic table with a cardboard tray holding two large cups with domed lids. It was mid-October, and yellow leaves covering the still-green grass were deep enough to kick. She and Dr. Michaels had met outside the coffee shop and agreed that he would cross the street to the park and save them a table. As always, it was a Friday afternoon. Tonya had called on Monday to ask if the professor had time to get together and talk.

"So, Tonya," he began, starting things off with a standard—but effective—opening, "how's it going?"

"Good, great—I don't know! That's one of the reasons I wanted to get together—other than to just say hello. It's been seven weeks. I'm hanging in there." Tonya threw her leg over the bench and sat down, resting her elbows on the table and twirling a perfect golden leaf.

Dr. Michaels lifted the dome off his latte and smiled at Tonya. "Let's go with your outline," he said. "What's good? What's great? And what don't you know?"

"Good are the school and the classes I'm teaching—beginning Spanish, pre-algebra, and one calculus section. No problem with the material, and the textbooks are good. Great would be the students—most of the time—great kids. They know I'm new and young, and they're curious about my heritage. Sometimes it takes a while to get them to settle down, and then I can lose them in a second. I get frustrated, but I find if I don't yell and wait patiently, they come back and pay attention. They do okay on the quizzes and most of them hand in homework. And," Tonya tossed her head and grinned at the professor, "you'll like this—they come right into the classroom. Maybe they don't *run* into the room, but they don't linger in the hall either."

The professor rewarded his protégé with a chuckle. "Do you know all their names?"

"Yes," Tonya responded. She'd been wanting him to ask. "That was one of my first challenges. And I had them learn the names of everyone in the class—first, middle, and last—and each person's favorite vegetable."

The professor tapped his fingers on the table and looked over at Tonya. "And why, may I ask, did you have them do that?"

Tonya realized he was playing along and continued the game. "I heard about it somewhere, a professor or something. It has to do with mastery learning. Once a student has learned all the names and vegetables, he realized he has accomplished something—he has mastered it. If he—or she—can do that, he can master Spanish verbs or algebraic functions. Plus," and she paused to take a sip of her coffee, "it builds community in the classroom. They get to know each other."

"And you show them you care about knowing them when you learn their names." Michaels taunted her with a grin, "Did you learn the vegetables, too?"

"Sure did," Tonya answered with enthusiasm. "And they all got involved pulling for each other because I told them when everyone knew all the names, they would have no weekend homework."

"I like that," the professor mused. "And what was your reward?"

"I could call everyone by name. It helped me get to know the individuals and set the tone for the classroom. It forced me to pay attention to them as much as to my exciting, brilliant lesson plans."

"Hail, hail, Ms. Simmons! Teacher extraordinaire!" Michaels stood with his cup to toast Tonya, then sat down and became serious. "So what is it you don't know?"

"I don't know if I'm really a teacher. Sometimes I think I'm lost, completely lost." Tonya looked as if she were about to cry. "It's overwhelming. Trees spring up everywhere, and I can't see—even imagine—the forest." She grimaced at the forest-for-the-trees image, but it conveyed exactly what she'd been experiencing. "There's record keeping, and discipline, and a lesson that didn't go well, and how to arrange the room, and a parent calls with a theory about language learning, and someone loses a textbook, and an assembly interrupts my plan for the week, and the overhead light burns out and one kid hurls this obnoxious slur at another kid who goes after him with a chair."

Dr. Michaels sipped his latte while Tonya collected herself. With the slightest of hand gestures, he encouraged her to go on.

"Some days," Tonya started up again, "I feel like a complete sham, like what am I doing there? It's minute-by-minute management. Crisis mode. All the stuff we talked about—commitment, expectations, visions—they just seem like empty abstractions. I can hardly remember which page I'm on in an algebra book, let alone work on making a difference. I'm just glad to have survived another day. What happened, Dr. Michaels? I wanted so much to be a teacher. Have I lost it?"

"No, Tonya." The professor's tone was kind but serious. "You haven't lost it. Obviously you care. You just said so." Michaels capped his latte and pushed it down the table with the back of his hand. "What you describe is reality. It happens to all of us at first. You'll get the hang of the details—all that administrative stuff. When you've been through it once, the second time is much easier. My ex-wife—she was an elementary school teacher—said it was like making a complicated dessert. The first time all those instructions seem impossible to coordinate with the measuring and the timing. The next time, you know what to anticipate, and it all falls into place—or at least it gets better. By the third or fourth time, it's second nature."

"I can see how that might be, but right now this teaching thing is beginning to feel more like a job than a 'noble profession.'" Three destroyed napkins lay in front of Tonya on the picnic table, and she was shredding a fourth. "And that worries me, too. My fiancé thinks I'm obsessed. I get up at four in the morning and start making notes for a new lesson. I fixate on the kids who act turned off. We go out for pizza with friends, and all I can talk about is what worked and what didn't work in my classes that day. Maybe I care too much! But I want to be a good teacher." Tonya turned on the bench, put her feet up, rested her chin on her knees and muttered, "I want to make a difference."

Dr. Michaels respected her frustration and waited a few minutes before offering his thoughts. "You are becoming a teacher, Tonya," he said, using his most reassuring teacher voice. "Becoming a teacher is a growth process. It never stops—as long as you are still committed and caring. You will grow in understanding your relationship with the students, you will grow through knowing who they are and what they need, you will grow by being in the world and paying attention. And you will grow by knowing yourself."

"But before I can be good, I have to be competent." Tonya turned toward the professor, let her feet fall back to the grass, and slid off her sandals.

"You can be both competent and good." He answered her unasked question. "The processes grow together. The more competent you become at managing the minute to minute, the freer you will become to do what you love—being a teacher." With an insider's grin, he added, "Right now, you're juggling. Too much anxiety, too little control. Try balancing. Remember the tennis balls and the racquet."

Tonya acknowledged his reference with a quick smile, then returned to her train of thought. "And then I wonder if I will ever know enough to be the resource they need, to meet their expectations for me." Tonya glanced at Dr. Michaels to be sure she had the okay to tell her story. "One girl, Carrie," she continued, "brought in an old birthday card her mother had received from an uncle in Mexico maybe 30 years ago. She asked me to translate the printed verse, and I didn't recognize all the words. I felt so foolish, like I had no right to be the teacher."

"So," goaded Michaels as he waited for Tonya to continue.

"So," mimicked Tonya, "I felt like a jerk."

"You didn't know a few words on a birthday card," Michaels said sarcastically, "that doesn't mean you have no knowledge—or even inadequate knowledge. You do have knowledge of teaching and learning—plus knowledge of Spanish. But you don't know everything. I don't know everything—hardly—and I'm twice your age!"

"I guess you're right, but still I felt like a sham." Tonya caught herself about to pout and shook her head to get rid of the expression. "There are kids in my calculus class who I swear are born geniuses. I have to study myself to keep up with their questions."

"And there is nothing wrong with that." The sun was warm on the professor's back. He rotated his stiff shoulders and flexed his fingers. "You grow as a teacher, it's a process. Knowledge is a process, too, and one of our goals as teachers is to turn students into active learners. What you don't know, you can learn. You can look up the words you don't know and add to you knowledge. Carrie can look them up, too. Then you both learn."

Tonya nodded her acknowledgment. "Actually," she told her professor, "that's what I did. And eventually we involved the whole class in translating the birthday note. We were detectives. It was real life. Like I think we said in your office, knowledge that works in the world, or learning that opens the world."

"I've always observed," the professor continued, "that the best teachers were the best students. They loved learning, and they never stopped. They continued to take courses in their field and in areas that intrigued them. They traveled and observed and couldn't wait to get back to their students to share all their new knowledge and discoveries. They didn't "teach" love of learning, they lived it— demonstrated it—and the students caught the message." Michaels realized he had lapsed into a minilecture, almost a sermon, but he was feeling passionate about learning and knowledge and teaching and, given the attentive audience, didn't want to stop when he was on a roll. This was a man who recognized an educable moment!

"Part of your growth as a teacher and in knowledge," he pressed on with conviction, "will be how you relate your teaching to the world. You will keep learning about the world because you want to gain knowledge. You will begin to see connections everywhere between what you want the students to learn and the world they live in. Environment issues can become algebra problems. Your students can develop a sense of familiarity with celebrities, politicians, or scientist from Spanish-speaking countries."

Tonya listened politely but looked as if she wanted to get back to her issues. Dr. Michaels caught her attention again with one of his examples. "Think of it this way. You are getting ready to buy your first new car. You study consumer magazines, visit lots, and finally decide on a Mazda Miata. It's yours. One afternoon you're driving home from work, and there's another car, just like yours, but blue. 'That's my car!' you announce to the car pool. It's a great moment." Michaels smiled at Tonya, waiting for the great ah-ha! It didn't come. Instead, she looked at him quizzically and asked, "What?"

"The car, the excitement." Michaels tried to be patient. "Now all other Mazda Miatas are your car, you have a personal connection with all those other Mazda drivers!"

"Oh." Tonya had a glint of recognition in her eyes. "Even just knowing some simple Spanish vocabulary can connect the kids to events happening in Mexico or Central America that they read about in the paper. The more we learn, the more connected we are." She paused and laughed, "Am I getting it, Professor?"

"Better than you think, Ms. Simmons. It's all a process, and you're fully into the flow." Again the professor turned serious. "How are you doing with the trees and the forest? Are you catching glimpses of the forest again?"

"It really does help to talk with someone who's been there." Tonya scowled with embarrassment but went ahead anyway. "It would be wonderful if every new teacher could have a mentor like you, some-one to talk with about the questions without any fear of appearing weak or foolish, or of it affecting evaluations or job security. Someone with wisdom."

"Why not? You did it, Tonya, you took responsibility for getting what you felt you needed. You came to my office with the questions and the commitment. You brought your offerings to the table, and we both gained. It would be good if you would encourage your new teacher friends to do the same, to find their own mentors. Then we older, more experienced but still learning teachers will be even more vested in the future of our profession. You've done that for me."

"But you are so wise," Tonya said, conscious that she was almost flirting but sincere nevertheless, "which leads me to ask, when does wisdom happen?"

"In some respects, you are quite wise now," the professor reas-sured her. Then he turned the question around to Tonya and asked, "What is wisdom, anyway?"

"Wisdom is what you do with knowledge, I guess." Tonya half kneeled on the bench, getting into the kind of discussion she loved. "First you get the knowledge from experience, then you use that knowledge. Knowing how to use what you've learned is wisdom. Making judgments based on what you know is wisdom."

"That's a good start." The professor was also taken with the discussion. "A wise teacher uses her knowledge in making the minute-to-minute decisions you were talking about earlier. She also uses her knowledge to apply what she knows to the big picture."

"So," Tonya interrupted, "the teacher passes on both knowledge and wisdom. What she knows and how she applies what she knows."

"And," Michaels added, keeping with the pace, "she keeps the trees and the forest in balance—what she knows and what she dreams of accomplishing."

"Sounds to me as if you're getting back to that vision exercise you had me do," Tonya pulled her wallet from the colorful bag she now carried instead of the old backpack. "I actually shrunk mine down to a small font and keep it in my wallet."

"Have you ever reread what you wrote?" the professor asked.

"No. No time. Too much to do right now to think about my vision."

"This is precisely the time when you need to check back with your vision and your expectations. You need to keep balance—perspective. You need to remember your vision when the trees, all that classroom stuff, close in." Michaels hesitated before going on. "When you were writing your vision, I went back and reconsidered mine." He didn't pull any folded paper from his wallet, but he seemed to be reading something in the sky over Tonya's shoulder. "I wanted my teaching to excite students to become learners. I wanted my students to love their world and their lives and gain as much knowledge as they could. I wanted them to become connected to the world and to each other through learning and caring." The professor wiped the back of his hand across his mouth and rested his elbows on the table, leaning toward Tonya with one of the most serious expression she had witnessed.

"Did revisiting your vision make a difference?" Tonya asked, already knowing the answer.

"First, I was appalled at how ordinary and, well, almost clichéd it sounded." He smiled apologetically. "But then I realized this wasn't a writing exercise. It was a personal note from me to me about my vision for my profession. After many years, I connected again with my purpose, my vision, and I got excited."

The professor seemed caught up in describing his rekindled energy. Tonya knew that to show she was a good listener, she should ask him more about his new enthusiasm, but she was forming a realization of her own and just had to express it.

"My vision, my mission," she announced as preliminary to her point, "that's the core of my problem." She looked to see if Michaels was with her—and he was. "I'm not doing it. I'm not teaching my vision, and that's why I wanted to be a teacher in the first place."

Dr. Michaels focused his full attention on Tonya. "You don't teach your vision, Tonya, and you don't have your students memorize your mission statement. The vision is yours, and it influences just about everything you do as a teacher. You don't teach your mission, you live it." He rolled back his shoulders again against the fading warmth of the October sun. "When you demonstrate how to reduce an economic issue to an algebraic formula—for simplicity and clarity—you are connecting what your students are learning to their understanding of the world. When you learn about farming advances in Spanish-speaking countries or about rain forest politics and you share your caring with your students, you are showing your way of relating to the world."

"I had a teacher in sixth grade," Tonya offered as a way of saying she understood, "who made us memorize Bloom's taxonomy, you know, the levels of learning. That isn't meaningful for students. That's a guide for teachers who want a touchstone for how they're presenting material and challenging students. I guess it's the same way with my vision. It is for me that I keep it in focus. The idea is that it should inform or inspire my teaching and that the students benefit as I act on my mission."

Tonya hesitated, not satisfied that she had covered all her concerns. "There's one more thing," she went on while she still had Michael's attention. "How will I know if I'm communicating my vision, if I am really succeeding in my mission?"

"Maybe you won't know for years, and in some cases you may never know. You can give a Spanish or a calculus test, but it is much more difficult to test for someone's love of learning or evaluate a person's way of relating to the world." Michaels tapped his pocket to check for his keys. "Teach by example, Ms. Simmons. You'll recognize the results. You're an observer, remember?"

Tonya collected the cups and stood up. "I'm not sure if this was a new conversation or a review session," she stated with a restored lightness, "but whatever it was, I feel a lot better. Already I'm thinking about Monday, and I'm excited to get back to my students. Maybe I don't love the job, but I sure love the challenge of being a teacher!"

"Good to catch up with your progress." The professor stood as well. "Please give me a call whenever."

"I appreciate that. I will, and thanks for today." As they walked back toward the coffee shop, Tonya tossed out one more concern.

"I really like your way of teaching, but I don't think I can do it like you do. For one thing, I don't have all your stories. And I want to try your ideas, but I can't deliver them like you do. I don't have your style. I wish I did, but I don't."

"You have your own style." The professor waited for a noisy painter's van to pass before he elaborated. "All good teachers don't look alike. In fact, good teachers vary enormously in their styles." He turned toward Tonya with his "get ready because I'm about to deliver" expression. "Remember last spring when we talked about Richard Traina and his research on what people valued in teachers they remembered?"

Tonya shrugged her shoulders to say she kind of remembered. Michaels continued anyway. "We were talking about caring that day, if I recall. Traina identified the three characteristics most often described by the Americans he had studied. They were, first, competence with the subject matter. Second, caring deeply about their student's success, and third, a distinctive character." He waited for Tonya to catch up, and when he saw that she was with him, he continued. "A distinctive character—your character, your style. What a waste of misplaced energy it would be for you to try to act like someone you aren't. Let your style reflect your values, your passions, your way of being. Your distinctive character will come from your honesty and sincerity, not from copying someone else." The professor paused before offering his final observation. "You have a style, Tonya, that is all yours. You're determined, a bit feisty, excitable, and confident—not overconfident or cocky, but confident in a way that generates respect. You like getting on with the adventure, and you will take your students with you." He allowed himself a self-satisfied smile for a fine professorial, or "mentorial," moment.

After waiting a few seconds for his message to settle, Dr. Michaels pushed the walk button on the streetlight.

"Let me leave you with a Michaels-ism," he said, interrupting the silence between them, "a realization I had one snowy night walking from the library to the student center. Students had created a path in the snow that went from the library to the center, as a bird would fly. I decided to make a new path with my own footprints. I wrote down my epiphany, and I offer it to you. 'If we believe in walking down life's beaten path, we will seldom make any tracks of our own.' He smiled at Tonya and then to himself as he turned toward his car.

Conversation Points

1. From a professional development perspective, what will you do to continue to improve your teaching strategies?

2. Are you a student *in* education or are you a student *of* education?

3. When will you follow the beaten path, and when will you make tracks of your own?

Recommended Readings

During my travels, I am often asked, "What do you read?" I typically rattle off a few books that I am currently in the middle of and let it go at that. Here is a selection of texts that I have read over the past 10 years. As you can see, the majority of the books are biographical or about people involved in personal triumph. Some of the books may not be "education" readings, but all of them focus on important lessons learned.

Piano Lessons: Music, Love, & True Adventures, Noah Adams
Tuesdays With Morrie, Mitch Albom
I Know Why the Caged Bird Sings, Maya Angelou
Days of Grace: A Memoir, Arthur Ashe and Arnold Rampersad
The Majic Bus: An American Odyssey, Douglas Brinkley
Living Loving & Learning, Leo F. Buscaglia
The Education of Little Tree, Forrest Carter
The Emperor of Ocean Park, Stephen L. Carter
The Water Is Wide, Pat Conroy
Bud, Not Buddy, Christopher Paul Curtis
Fires in the Bathroom: Advice for Teachers From High School Students, Kathleen Cushman
The Art of Happiness: A Handbook for Living, His Holiness the Dalai Lama and Howard C. Cutler, MD
A Lesson Before Dying: A Novel, Ernest J. Gaines
My Side of the Mountain, Jean Craighead George
Roots, Alex Haley
Standing at the Scratch Line: A Novel, Guy Johnson
Q: The Autobiography of Quincy Jones, Quincy Jones
Vernon Can Read!: A Memoir, Vernon E. Jordan, Jr., with Annette Gordon-Reed
There Are No Children Here: The Story of Two Boys Growing Up in the Other America, Alex Kotlowitz
Savage Inequalities: Children in America's Schools, Jonathon Kozol

The Autobiography of Malcom X as Told to Alex Haley, Malcolm X and
   Alex Haley
Long Walk to Freedom, Nelson Mandela
Life of Pi, Yann Martel
*Kaffir Boy: The True Story of a Black Youth's Coming of Age in Apartheid
   South Africa,* Mark Mathabane
Escalante: The Best Teacher in America, Jay Mathews
Makes Me Wanna Holler: A Young Black Man in America, Nathan McCall
I, Rigoberta Menchu: An Indian Woman in Guatemala, Rigoberta Menchu
The Way of the Peaceful Warrior: A Book That Changes Lives, Dan
   Millman
Talking to High Monks in the Snow: An Asian American Odyssey, Lydia
   Minatoya
*The Tao of Teaching: The Special Meaning of the Tao Te Ching as Related
   to the Art of Teaching,* Greta K. Nagel
*The Challenge to Care in Schools: An Alternative Approach to Education
   (Contemporary Educational Thought),* Nel Noddings
Let the Trumpet Sound: The Life of Martin Luther King, Jr., Stephen B. Oats
White Teacher, Vivian Gussin Paley
The Measure of a Man: A Spiritual Autobiography, Sydney Poitier
You Have to Go to School, You're the Teacher, Renee Rosenblum-Lowden
Blindness, Jose Saramago
Do What You Love, the Money Will Follow: Discovering Your Right Livelihood,
   Masha Sinetar
"What Makes A Good Teacher?" *Education Week, 18*(19), Richard P. Traina
The Color Purple, Alice Walker

Index

DATE DUE	
MAR 0 2 2008	